This is an inspiring story of love and commitment. It's the kind of story Jesus would have told to his friends. You'll learn a little more about the power of love in these pages.

BOB GOFF
New York Times bestselling author of *Love Does*

When I met Justin and Patrick and heard their story, I cried, and I wanted everyone I knew to hear this important story. We live in a culture that values romantic love and to a certain extent familial love, but we have very few stories of brotherhood like this one: a story about lifelong friends who, when life became challenging, didn't back away, but instead became more committed to one another, more connected, more willing to sacrifice. This is an important, beautiful, inspiring story.

SHAUNA NIEQUIST
New York Times bestselling author of *Present over Perfect* and *Bread & Wine*

I'll Push You is not just the remarkable story of one able-bodied man pushing another man's wheelchair on a five-hundred-mile journey. It's the story of two friends who've spent their entire life's journey pushing each other to be better people. Through their courage, grace, and dignity, Justin and Patrick remind us that we are stronger together than separate. As it turns out, we all need a push.

MEREDITH VIEIRA
Journalist and talk show host

In our fast-paced world of shallow engagement, *I'll Push You* comes as a breath of fresh air, depicting a brotherly friendship that is refreshingly deep and authentic. Disarmingly vulnerable and dangerously challenging, Patrick and Justin offer us a glimpse of what true friendship can look like if we're willing to take the risks.

TIM FOREMAN
Bassist for Switchfoot

I'll Push You is a powerful story of friendship and faith, defining what it means to be a part of a community. The love that is so evident in Justin and Patrick's story is a brilliant reminder of how we should engage with one another, a reminder of what the church is meant to be.

JEREMY COWART
Photographer and founder of The Purpose Hotel

I'LL

A JOURNEY *OF* 500 MILES,

PUSH

TWO BEST FRIENDS, *AND* ONE WHEELCHAIR

YOU

PATRICK GRAY *AND* JUSTIN SKEESUCK

TYNDALE
MOMENTUM™

The nonfiction imprint of
Tyndale House Publishers, Inc.

EL CAMINO DE SANTIAGO
CAMINO FRANCÉS (THE "FRENCH WAY")

GALICIA

SANTIAGO DE COMPOSTELA

Arzúa

A Brea

Monumento de Monte do Gozo

Palas de Rei

Portomarín

Sarria

Triacastela

O Cebreiro

Villafranca del Bierzo

Molinaseca

Rabanal del Camino

† *Cruz de Ferro*

Astorga

Villavante

ESPAÑA

LEÓN

El Burgo R

T H E   M

PORTUGAL

GOLFO DE
VIZCAYA

TO PARIS

FRANCE

Bayonne

St. Jean Pied de Port

Roncesvalles

THE PYRENEES

PAMPLONA
SKIP

*Front wheel
breaks off*

Alto de Perdón

Estella

Obanos

Los Arcos

NAVARRA

Santo Domingo
de la Calzada

Hontanas

Belorado

Nájera

LOGROÑO

Carrión de
los Condes

San Juan
de Ortega

LA RIOJA

Ila
eza

Boadilla
del Camino

*Hill outside
Castrojeriz*

BURGOS

S E T A

STILLIA Y LEON

N

0   25   50   100km

Our 500-mile journey

Visit Tyndale online at www.tyndale.com.

Visit Tyndale Momentum online at www.tyndalemomentum.com.

TYNDALE, *Tyndale Momentum*, and Tyndale's quill logo are registered trademarks of Tyndale House Publishers, Inc. The Tyndale Momentum logo is a trademark of Tyndale House Publishers, Inc. Tyndale Momentum is the nonfiction imprint of Tyndale House Publishers, Inc., Carol Stream, Illinois.

I'll Push You: A Journey of 500 Miles, Two Best Friends, and One Wheelchair

Designed by Justin Skeesuck

Published in association with The Christopher Ferebee Agency; www.christopherferebee.com.

Scripture quotations are paraphrased by the authors.

In chapter 17, Claudia's journal entry is used with her permission. She retains all rights.

Names and other identifying details of some individuals have been changed to protect their privacy.

For information about special discounts for bulk purchases, please contact Tyndale House Publishers at csresponse@tyndale.com, or call 1-800-323-9400.

ISBN 978-1-4964-2169-2 (hc)
ISBN 978-1-4964-2170-8 (sc)

Printed in the United States of America

23 22 21 20 19 18 17
7   6   5   4

— TO OUR WIVES —

Thank you for loving us,
for laughing with us (and often at us),
and for rolling your eyes at only half our jokes.

— TO OUR CHILDREN —

Remember, it's only impossible
because you haven't done it yet, so dream big!

CONTENTS

FOREWORD

— Donald Miller —

As a writer, I have spent much of my adult life studying stories—exploring the art of creating them, examining their structure, striving to perfect the practice of telling them. And through my years of studying, writing, and telling stories, I have fallen in love with many. Some of my favorites are stories of victims choosing to be heroes, of individuals redeeming their suffering, and of incredible shared journeys. Frequently these stories challenge me to look at myself differently; they change my perspective of the world around me. Too often, though, these stories are crafted by the imagination of man, engineered by longings of the heart, and designed by desires of the soul. Rarely have I encountered such a story lived out in the everyday, where the hero—or in this case, heroes—could easily be you and me, ordinary people choosing to embrace an extraordinary life.

When I first met Justin Skeesuck and Patrick Gray, I knew something was different about them. These two men were filled with a passion for life and a desire to share a remarkable hope with all they encounter. But it wasn't until I knew their story that I truly appreciated their friendship and understood how much hope and power there can be in our relationships.

I came across the story recounted in *I'll Push You* in October 2015, a little over a year after these two men accomplished what many had said would be impossible. While their five-hundred-mile wheelchair journey through Spain is truly incredible, the most powerful part of their adventure is the undying and relentless nature of the love they possess for each other.

All too often, men shy away from intimacy, or run from being vulnerable. However, these two have redefined what friendship means. They have challenged conventional views of what a relationship can be, and in doing so, challenge many traditional concepts. Their deep friendship has kept them from being victims, has given them the opportunity to redeem any suffering they have experienced, and has allowed a beautiful adventure of life to unfold.

The story within these pages reminds us that God didn't create us to live alone. He never meant us to be solitary creatures. *I'll Push You* demonstrates what it means to live in community with one another and reveals what can happen when we shoulder each other's burdens. Justin and Patrick demonstrate the beauty that exists when we choose to be the hands and feet we are called to be. They show us the redeeming power that exists in giving others the opportunity to love all of who we are, in spite of our flaws and imperfections.

Be careful! When you choose to read this incredible testament of life, friendship, and faith, you will be challenged and will begin to look for those adventures that are already part of your life, the ones you haven't embraced. Not the five-hundred-mile journeys through foreign countries, but the unbound nature of living we are all capable of experiencing when we let our relationships be all they are meant to be.

Welcome to *I'll Push You.*

PROLOGUE

A CLOUDLESS EXPANSE OF blue stretches as far as I can see. Distant hills are covered in grasses of green and gold. Several trees cast long shadows across the dirt and stones at their base, and the shrill notes of songbirds in the branches punctuate the silence. Their song brings me back to the voice inside my head.

So much beauty and yet so much pain.

My body is covered in sweat, and though my hands feel weak, they are the least of my worries.

How much more can my body take? . . . Is this it? . . . Have I reached the end of what I can do?

With every step, my legs feel heavier. The pain in my calves throbs. I just want it to stop . . . please make it stop.

More time. I thought I had more time.

I was afraid this would happen, but I thought it wouldn't catch up with me until the very end. Now, it's all I can do to take ten steps before I'm forced to rest.

Just steady yourself and push through the pain.

The ache spreads to my thighs, and my calves begin to quiver before I can take eight more steps.

Rest . . . just a few minutes of rest.

I decide to keep moving, but after five more steps, the pain is almost unbearable and the weakness is spreading. I extend my right leg back to stretch my calf muscles. This offers a momentary reprieve from the pain. The slight relief I feel as I stretch my left leg tells me I can keep going, but after three more steps, I find out how wrong I am. This is it—my legs won't carry me any farther.

Why is this happening now?

I find a place to sit, but the pain continues. My jaw clenches as I fight back the urge to scream out my frustration. My hands curl into fists as anger wells up within me. Fully spent, I want to release the exhaustion, the frustration, and the pain.

My body is failing me. Even worse, *I'm* failing—my wife, my kids, my friends.

All my life, I've been in control. Now . . . I feel it slipping away.

— PART I —

BEGINNINGS

1
ANSWERS AND QUESTIONS

How MANY HOURS HAVE I spent in the waiting room of a doctor's office over the past thirteen years? I've lost count. During that time, I've endured an unending series of muscle biopsies, MRIs, blood tests, and various other forms of poking, probing, and prodding. And still no diagnosis I can depend on.

When I was in high school, my best friend, Patrick Gray, used to come with me to a lot of my appointments, but the distance between his home in Idaho and mine in Southern California makes that a little difficult now. Since moving to San Diego, I've often sat here alone, waiting for answers. Today, I'm grateful that my wife, Kirstin, is able to be with me.

The door leading back to the exam rooms opens, and Jennifer, my doctor's medical assistant, surveys the busy waiting room. We make eye contact, and even though she knows Kirstin and me well, she goes through the formality of calling my name.

"Justin Skeesuck, come on back."

By the time I get to my feet, with my leg braces and cane keeping me upright, Kirstin is already at the door. She knows I want to get

3

there on my own, even if it takes me a while. As we continue down the hall, Kirstin and Jennifer slow their gait to allow me to keep up.

"I like your cane, Justin," Jennifer says as we approach the exam room. "Is it new?"

I look down at the dark purple wood. "Yeah, my best friend made it for me."

"It's beautiful."

When the weakness spread from my left leg to my right, Patrick purchased a four-foot slab of purpleheart wood and spent hours in his garage with a jigsaw and hand sanding tools, fashioning a beautiful cane. It has become a cherished symbol of our lifelong friendship.

"The doctor will be with you in a few minutes," Jennifer says as my wife and I take our seats. Smiling, she closes the door softly.

Kirstin has come prepared for the wait. She pulls a magazine out of her purse and begins to thumb through the pages to pass the time. I settle into my chair, lean my head back against the wall, and close my eyes as time seems to stand still.

"It's taking longer than normal," Kirstin says after a while, as she replaces the magazine in her purse.

"There were a lot of people in the waiting room today," I reply. "I'm just hoping that when he gets here he has some answers this time."

For years, my team of neurologists has struggled to identify what exactly is going on in my body. Though my symptoms are similar to those of some well-known diseases—such as ALS— they don't perfectly align with any of them. We're hoping this latest round of tests, blood work, and muscle biopsies will bring a breakthrough—anything that will give me some insight into what the future might hold.

I would be satisfied at this point just to have a name for what I have. My team of physicians has gone through four diagnoses so far, and all have proved to be incorrect. Whatever I have is so rare, they aren't sure it even *has* a name.

The doctor finally walks in and takes a seat on the rolling stool. His white lab coat hangs loosely over a tweed sport coat, and his salt-and-pepper hair is combed neatly. He glances at my chart in his hands and looks at Kirstin and me through his large, metal-rimmed glasses.

"Hey, guys, how are you doing today?" he says with a faint hint of a smile.

"Hoping for some answers," I reply with a chuckle, "but expecting more questions."

"Fair enough. Well, today we have a little bit of both."

Never one for chitchat, he quickly begins his exam. Working his way from head to toe, he checks my eyes, listens to my heart and lungs, checks my blood pressure, tests my reflexes, and probes for any pain in my joints. He finishes the exam by testing my hand strength to make sure the weakness hasn't spread.

Seemingly satisfied, he says, "Let's head down the hall."

We follow him, as we have dozens of times before, to finish my appointment in the quiet of his office, a surprisingly small space filled with a large desk in the center surrounded by walls of bookshelves full of medical journals and books with names I can't pronounce. His diploma from Harvard and several framed awards have a prominent place on the wall.

"We've never been more certain of a diagnosis than we are now," he says as he settles into his desk chair and we sit down across from him.

"All right," I say. "Does it have a name?"

5

The doctor's face tightens almost imperceptibly. "We're pretty certain you have what is called multifocal acquired motor axonopathy. Or MAMA for short."

"What exactly is it?" Kirstin asks.

"It's similar in many respects to ALS. Which is why Justin was misdiagnosed the first time around."

Turning to me, he continues, "Your immune system is attacking your nervous system, and your motor nerves are shutting down. This disease doesn't affect your sensory nerves, just your ability to move. Normally, it hinders limited portions of a person's body, but in your case, it has attacked everything from your waist down. That's one of the reasons you've been so difficult to diagnose. MAMA typically starts in the hands. To see it affect such a large portion of the body is quite rare."

My wife leans forward and grabs my hand. "Will it get worse? Do we know how long we have?"

"Like I said, we have both answers *and* questions today . . ."

He pauses for a moment before continuing.

"It will get worse over time. To what degree, we still aren't sure."

"So, what's the deal?" I ask.

"It's likely this disease will result in complications that will lead to your death."

Kirstin takes a slow, deep breath as her eyes well up with tears.

This isn't the first time I've been told I'm going to die. When I was originally diagnosed with ALS, the doctor told me I had four years to live. That was nearly nine years ago. This time there's no known life expectancy, but the prognosis feels different; it feels more real.

"Do we know what causes it?" I ask.

"Well, we don't know precise cause and effect, but sometimes traumatic events can trigger certain diseases."

He pauses again to gather his thoughts and then continues. "Our best guess is that the disease was dormant throughout your childhood, and that it may have been awakened by your car accident."

"What?"

That accident was thirteen years ago.

| | |

It was a crisp, clear spring morning in April 1991, but I remember it like it was yesterday. The brilliant blue sky over my hometown of Ontario, Oregon, was devoid of clouds, and the rising sun sat low, just above the horizon to the east, making silhouettes of the mountains as I stepped outside my front door to wait for my friend Jason to pick me up for a basketball tournament that was scheduled to start in less than an hour.

"Where is he?" I wondered aloud. "We're going to be late."

As if on cue, Jason rounded the corner in his small, dark red 1987 Toyota pickup. I poked my head back inside the house to say good-bye to my parents before walking out to the driveway, where Jason was now waiting.

A few months shy of my sixteenth birthday, I was still too young to drive, but Jason had recently gotten his license, and he was eager to get his well-traveled truck out on the freeway. As I fastened my seatbelt across my chest and lap, I looked over at Jason. His lap belt was secure, but the shoulder strap was hanging loose.

"You should probably get that fixed," I said with a raised eyebrow. Jason just smiled and put the truck in gear.

In a matter of minutes, we were on I-84, headed east toward Northwest Nazarene College in nearby Nampa, Idaho. Even with our sunglasses on, the rising sun made us squint as it filled the gap between the pickup's sun visors and the mountains in the distance. Because we were running late, Jason put some extra weight to the gas pedal.

As the sun climbed a little higher in the sky, the glare from the east intensified. At 80 mph, Jason was doing his best to get us to the gymnasium on time. But the faster he went, the more noticeable the poor alignment of his truck became.

As I leaned forward to find some good music on the radio, the twist of the dial was interrupted by a loud *thump, thump, thump* from under my feet.

Looking up, I saw we had drifted hard to the right and both passenger-side tires were off the edge of the asphalt, bouncing through the dirt, gravel, and tufts of grass on the poorly maintained shoulder. As Jason struggled for control, I could see we were rapidly approaching a concrete support pillar of an overpass.

"Jason, look out!"

He jerked the wheel hard to the left, trying to get us back onto the roadway, but overcorrected, sending the truck into a 180-degree spin. For a split second, we were facing west, with traffic speeding toward us—until we slid onto the median and began to roll. The explosive sound of metal on gravel filled my ears as the truck slammed against the ground. Everything happened so fast, I soon lost my bearings as we rolled across the median and caught some air.

It was a brief moment, but time stood still.

So many thoughts rushed through my head as the ground outside my window came at me in slow motion. When the passenger side of the truck collided with the ground one last time, the sound was deafening, and the impact reverberated throughout my body.

Is this how my life will end?

What will the paramedics tell my family?

What will my parents say to Patrick?

When the truck finally came to rest, I was suspended from my seat by my seatbelt and Jason was below me, with his upper body partially out the window of the driver side door, the door frame across his back. A small depression in the ground was all that kept the truck from crushing him.

Looking out through the fractured windshield, I could see multiple vehicles stopped in the distance and many people running toward us to help.

"Jason, are you alive?"

"Yes," came his muffled reply, as his upper body was trapped between the truck and the ground below.

"I have to get out of here!" I yelled as I kicked at the windshield, but it wouldn't budge.

Desperate to help my friend, I unbuckled my seatbelt and tumbled down on top of him. I heard him moan in pain.

"Get off me!" he said through gritted teeth.

I shifted my feet and straddled his body while pushing against the passenger door above me. It didn't move. Somehow, though, I was able to wiggle my way out through the slider in the rear window.

As my feet touched the ground, several people approached me. I shouted, "My friend is still trapped! He needs help!"

Someone yelled, "Let's see if we can get the truck back on its wheels."

With a collective effort, the assembled onlookers were able to heave the truck up high enough for Jason to pull himself back into the cab and release his seatbelt. As they continued to hold the truck off the ground, Jason was able to crawl out the driver's side window.

Somehow, I walked away from the accident with only a few scrapes and bruises. Jason wasn't as lucky. He ruptured some discs in his back. But considering the severity of the accident, his injuries could have been much worse.

Four months later, at the beginning of my junior year, I was running down the soccer field during a game when I noticed that my left foot wasn't moving normally. I could plant and push off to make a cut, but I couldn't raise my foot back up. No matter how hard I tried to control it, my foot would flop around. Sometimes the toe of my cleats caught the ground as I ran, causing me to stumble.

When I brought this to my parents' attention, we began looking for answers. The problem seemed to be isolated to my foot, so we went to a podiatrist. He was completely stumped and referred us to a neurologist. The neurologist had no real answers, but he had a plaster cast molding made of my left foot, which resulted in a custom-fitted white orthotic brace made of lightweight plastic. This new support was a foot bed insert for my shoes that curved around my heel and snugly supported my calf. This brace provided the support needed to maintain a relatively normal level of activity.

For one of my fitting appointments, Patrick went with me.

As I stood up and took a few steps with the brace securely

fastened across the front of my lower leg with a Velcro strap, the aluminum hinges on each side of my ankle squeaked.

"Dude! You can totally play the sympathy card with the ladies!" Patrick said with a laugh.

Raising my eyebrows, I replied, "Not a bad idea!"

"How does it feel?" he asked as I walked around the doctor's office.

"Better than dragging my foot."

"I kind of like you dragging your foot," he said, chuckling to himself. "Makes me look better!"

"You're an idiot," I said, laughing out loud.

"Seriously though, you're moving pretty well. I can barely see a limp."

Running a few steps, I felt my confidence rising. "Yeah! It feels great. I think I can still play tennis with no problem."

With this new support system, I took up my racket and played both my junior and senior years. I kept close tabs on the weakness in my foot, and it seemed the worst was over. But not long after graduation, I could feel it spreading to more muscles in my lower leg.

| | |

I'd never made the connection between the weakness in my legs and the accident—until now. Kirstin is still sitting quietly next to me, holding my hand tightly. I'm squeezing hers so hard I can feel her pulse against my palm. So many thoughts are racing through my mind.

Turning to me, my wife says, "You need to call Patrick."

2
PHONE CALLS

— PATRICK —

IT'S A GORGEOUS DAY IN MAY, with crystal clear skies, but I'm stuck at home studying for an exam. The warm rays of light pouring through my office window make it difficult to focus. When the phone rings, I welcome the distraction. I could use a break from reading about "nursing management in the hospital setting."

A quick glance at the caller ID lifts my spirits. It's my best friend, Justin, calling from San Diego. He and I have known each other our entire lives, and even though we live a thousand miles apart, rarely a week or two goes by without one of us calling to keep in touch.

"Hello?"

"PAA-DDY!"

I can't help but laugh. I've heard Justin call out that name a thousand times in his usual singsong way, and every time it makes me smile.

"What's going on, Skeez? It's only been a few days since we talked. Is everything okay?"

As we continue to talk, I get up from my desk and head into

the kitchen. With the phone wedged between my shoulder and my ear, I pour myself a glass of water as I wait for him to reply.

In a calm voice, he says, "Yes and no."

"Is your family okay?"

"Yeah, yeah. Kirstin and Jaden are fine . . ."

He pauses and I grab the phone with my free hand, pressing it harder against my ear so I don't miss anything.

"I had an appointment with my neurologist this morning," Justin continues. "I have a diagnosis, and I think this one is going to stick."

"What is it?"

"They're saying it's multifocal acquired motor axonopathy."

"Whoa, that's a mouthful!"

"They call it MAMA for short."

As Justin recounts the details of his visit to the doctor, I return to my office. I'm surprised at how easy it is for him to talk about his illness, but then Justin has always been a glass-half-full kind of guy.

"So, what's the prognosis?" I ask.

"My doctor says the details of progression are unknown . . . but it will probably cut my life short."

"When?" I ask, my stomach tightening.

"No one knows."

Shaking slightly, I set the glass on my desk and sit down. Suddenly, the rays of sunshine streaming through my window seem less bright . . . less warm.

We talk for almost an hour before hanging up, and despite the fear and frustration, Justin's optimism never wavers.

When my wife, Donna, comes home from work, I tell her about my conversation with Justin.

"How long do they say he has?"

"They're not sure. It could be five years . . . could be twenty. No one really knows."

"How are you doing?" she asks as she puts her arms around my waist, pulling me close.

"I don't know." With Donna's head against my chest, my words come slowly. "I just keep wondering how much longer he'll be able to do his graphic design work . . . how he and Kirstin will make ends meet . . . how long he'll be able to drive. And if he dies, what will Kirstin do? What will happen to Jaden?"

Donna whispers, "I'm so sorry."

"I just wish I could spend more time with him."

| | |

Justin and I have known each other literally our entire lives. Born two days apart in the same hospital in July 1975, we grew up within a mile and a half of each other in the small eastern Oregon town of Ontario—an arid farming community where the only trees are those intentionally planted in yards or parks, or ones growing along the banks of the Snake River. When the summer winds blow, dust devils create spiraling brown clouds that rise into the air from nearby fields or vacant lots. But even though our surroundings weren't the most lush, verdant place on God's green earth, small-town life provided an ample supply of freedom and open space for two imaginative boys to create worlds where anything was possible.

My childhood home was on a dead-end street that backed up to an empty field with acres of dirt and weeds. Directly south, on the other side of the street, sat the white brick Nazarene church our families attended, surrounded by more acres of empty fields.

Along with our friends Greg and Bryan, and my younger brother, Michael, Justin and I spent hours digging holes, building forts, and imagining life-threatening scenarios of rescues behind enemy lines. Sticks became guns, folded blades of cheatgrass became knives, rocks were grenades, and outstretched hands made for a great force field.

Behind Justin's house, across town, sat the Deep Dirt Hills, a collection of trees, dirt mounds, and tufts of grass straight out of a *Calvin and Hobbes* comic strip. During the winter, when a blanket of snow covered the dormant grass and barren soil, we put on our winter coats, snow pants, boots, and gloves, and with stocking caps pulled low, down to our eyes, we headed out for adventure.

With round red saucers and inner tubes at the ready, we dove down the steep embankment into the canyon below. Trees rushed past—streaks of green and brown—as we leaned first to the left and then to the right, dodging rocks and bare patches that littered our path, until we finally made it to the bottom. But as we gathered our sleds and tubes and began the climb back to the top, it sure seemed as if we'd traveled much farther than we had.

Though the canyon was a fabrication, and the villains we fought with our makeshift weapons were figments of our imagination, the muscles of creativity grew strong and the adventures we shared cemented us together. Whether our exploits were real or imaginary, it didn't matter. Together we lived for the next adventure.

As we grew older, our adventures shifted from open fields to athletic fields. Though we were unspectacular athletes, to say the least, we both loved being active, and we shared a competitive streak that often exceeded our abilities. In high school, I ran track and played baseball, and we both played football. Justin played soccer, but tennis was really his game. He had been playing it since fifth grade and absolutely loved it. When he started having problems with his foot during our junior and senior years, he never gave up. He just tried harder.

During his freshman year of college, he tried out for the tennis team. Though he couldn't keep up with the other players, he still played recreationally. But right before Christmas break, he called to tell me he had given up tennis altogether.

"I'm giving my racket to my sister."

"You really can't play anymore?"

"I can still run, but the stepping from side to side is just too much for my left leg. When I shuffle laterally, I stumble and fall."

"How are you handling it?"

"I have my moments, but I'm okay. At least I can still run."

A few months later, when I called Justin to check in, he greeted me with more bad news.

"I can't run anymore."

"What happened? Are your legs just too weak?"

"Yeah, I was down at the track for a run, and they just gave out on me."

"Oh man, first tennis, and now this. . . . I'm so sorry."

"It's okay, but I already miss the air rushing past my face and the freedom of controlling how fast I can go," he admitted. "But what can I do?"

"Man, you're handling this a lot better than I would. I'd be angry."

"I do get angry, but it never helps. And I can still get around . . ."

The next year, Justin called to tell me his legs had grown so weak that walking long distances was a challenge. Though he could still drive, walking to and from his car was wearing him down.

"Well, I finally got a handicap parking pass," he said, sounding more upbeat than I would have expected. We had talked about how this might someday become necessary, but for a guy who used to run through the fields behind the church with me and race up and down hills on our sleds, to now be dependent on blue parking spaces because his legs had grown so weak, this seemed too much.

"You've had to give up a lot of independence. First your racket, then running, and now you need a handicap parking pass. . . . It never ceases to amaze me how well you're handling all of it. Sometimes I think I'm having a harder time with this than you are."

"It's definitely hard," he said, "but dwelling on the things I can't do anymore just eats away at me. I can't go there—at least not for long. There's still plenty I *can* do, and that's what I'm going to focus on."

A few seconds of silence passed while I tried to take in everything Justin was telling me. I gripped the phone tighter and told him the only thing I could think to say.

"Skeez, whatever you need, I'm here."

I'LL PUSH YOU

— JUSTIN —

IT'S A BEAUTIFUL, lazy San Diego Saturday in March 2012. I'm alone in my living room with the TV remote braced against my leg. Though I can no longer open doors, hold a cup to my lips, or button my shirt, I can still somehow manage to use the remote. Every bit of independence is precious. I take what I can get.

My boys, Jaden and Noah, are playing in the backyard, probably stirring up trouble. My daughter, Lauren, is in her bedroom singing, and Kirstin is tidying up in the kitchen. In the relative, and rare, quiet of the house, I turn on the television and begin flipping through the channels until I see European travel guru Rick Steves on PBS. Every time I've gone to Europe, his knowledge, wisdom, and travel advice has come in handy.

In 2001, Kirstin and I, along with Patrick and his wife, Donna, spent nearly a month traveling through Europe together. We flew into Paris, and then explored Switzerland, Austria, Germany, and Belgium by train. I had braces on both of my legs by that point, but I still had enough strength to walk shorter distances with my wife and friends. It's been almost eleven years since that trip, but the memories are still vivid. Though finances were tight for both us and the Grays at the time, we knew we had to go, and we made it happen, even working extra jobs and extra shifts to cover the expenses.

So what does Rick have for the world of channel surfers and public broadcast junkies today? Northern Spain? Sure, I haven't been there yet.

I watch as Steves explores the city of Pamplona, where the Fiesta de San Fermín (known for the running of the bulls) is an annual event, and describes Ernest Hemingway's influence on the culture there, dating back to the publication of *The Sun Also Rises* in 1926.

It's all very familiar until he mentions the Camino de Santiago, or Way of Saint James, a nearly 800-kilometer pilgrimage route beginning in the picturesque Basque village of St. Jean Pied de Port, about five miles across the French border, and ending at the cathedral in Santiago de Compostela, where the apostle James's bones are said to be buried.

As Steves takes me over the Pyrenees Mountains, through the flat plains of northern Spain, and across two more mountain ranges to the region of Galicia in northwestern Spain, I am completely captivated. And as I watch the images of hundreds of pilgrims trekking along this ancient pathway, a thought occurs to me.

I wonder if I could do that in my wheelchair.

For the past few years, Patrick and I have been looking for the perfect "guy trip" that we could do together. We've tossed around the idea of going to Germany for Oktoberfest, touring the East Coast, or even just hanging out on a tropical island somewhere; but for some reason the right trip hasn't revealed itself yet. Now as Rick unveils the Camino de Santiago, it hits me: *This is the trip Patrick and I need to take.* I haven't felt this sure of anything since the day I realized I had met "the one."

| | |

Kirstin and I first met a week or two after I graduated from college. When people ask me, I always say we met at a liquor store across the street from my apartment. It was actually more like a mini-mart where you could buy groceries, but the sign on the building just said *Liquor*, and frankly, it makes for a more interesting story.

The first time we met, I was wearing shorts and my calf-high braces were clearly visible, so it was obvious there was something wrong with my legs.

"Don't we go to the same church?" I asked. I think she thought it was some sort of pickup line, but at least it got the conversation started. After we talked for a few minutes, I smiled and said, "Well, I'll see you around."

The next week, I saw her again—*at church.* And a few days after that, I was delivering an ad I had designed for a taco shop, and she jogged right past me.

That's the third time I've seen this girl in less than two weeks, I thought. *Maybe I should ask her out.*

So I did.

And she said yes!

On our first date, we went to Casa de Pico in Old Town San Diego. I started the evening by saying, "I have a progressive neuromuscular disease, and I don't know how much time I have left, but I thought you should know about it up front."

There. It's out there. Let's see how she responds.

She paused for a second. "Oh."

I held my breath, bracing for the inevitable awkwardness. Instead, the corners of her mouth turned up into a warm smile, and she simply said, "Okay."

That's when I knew.

She was the one.

| | |

"Honey, could you come here please?"

"What's up?" Kirstin asks as she walks in from the kitchen.

"I want to show you something," I say, nodding my head toward the TV.

She sits on the sofa next to me. "What's this?" she asks. "Rick Steves?"

"Just watch for a minute," I say. Kirstin knows I'm always looking for new places we can explore together. It's one of the ways we've learned to deal with my disease over the years— grabbing every opportunity to make the most of life while I'm still able.

"What do you think?" I ask when the episode ends.

"What do you mean?"

"I wonder if I could do that in my wheelchair?"

She looks at me and without the slightest pause, says, "Why not? If it's something you want to do, then do it!"

This is one of the many things I love about my wife. No matter how crazy my ideas may be, no matter how unrealistic they seem, she never lets me shy away from pursuing them.

Now the only question is, *What will Patrick think?*

| | |

Two weeks later, Patrick, Donna, and their kids, Cambia, Joshua, and Olivia, arrive at our house for our annual get-together.

"They're here!" my kids shout as the Grays pull into the driveway in their minivan. After hugs are distributed all around and the luggage is deposited in the bedrooms, the kids run off to the backyard to blow off some pent-up energy, and Donna and Kirstin retreat to the dining room to catch up on each other's lives.

"Let's head into the living room," I say to Patrick. "There's something I want to show you."

He smiles and follows me into the other room. As he takes a seat on the chair next to me, he reaches over and places the television remote in my lap.

I click the power button and begin searching for the Rick Steves episode I recorded.

I'm wondering how Patrick will respond. We've both had some pretty wild ideas over the years, but going almost five hundred miles in a wheelchair through a foreign country is definitely at the top of the crazy scale.

I start the episode, and we watch in silence. I keep glancing over at Patrick, trying to get a feel for what's going through his mind. I can tell he's interested, but clearly he has no idea what I'm about to ask.

When the show finally ends, I turn off the TV and get right to the point.

"So, do you want to go across five hundred miles of northern Spain with me?"

Patrick just stares back at me. For all the years I've known him, this is one of the few times in our lives when I haven't been able to read him.

Is he in or is he out?

Do I even know what I am asking of him?

We've had so many adventures in the past, but nothing like this.

I don't know if what I'm asking is even possible, but I do know this—I can't imagine attempting it with anyone else.

When he finally opens his mouth to speak, he utters the three words that will change the course of our lives.

"I'll push you."

— PART II —

PREPARATIONS

4
TIME OFF

— PATRICK —

JUNE IS A BEAUTIFUL month in Meridian, Idaho. The sky is often bright blue, and the grass is brilliant green. Sprinklers run, flowers are in bloom, and folks spend many hours outdoors, basking in the sun.

Today is no exception. A light breeze counters the heat as my kids run through the playground of Kleiner Park. Some of my coworkers' children vie for a spot on the monkey bars while others play a game of tag with my oldest daughter, Cambria. A lanky eight-year-old, her long blonde hair trails behind her as my four-year-old son, Josh, struggles to match her long strides. Olivia, three, is in my wife's arms. She has adjusted well to life in America since her adoption from China, but big crowds still make her nervous. Life in the Chinese orphanage wasn't easy, and Donna's arms are the one place she always feels safe.

Donna makes small talk with a few new acquaintances as more people from my team at St. Luke's Hospital show up with their families. We've come for a break from the workday pressures and some well-earned leisure time at this late-spring barbecue. My boss, Ed, arrives with his family, and I see him walking toward the covered park benches where a row of coolers and dishes full of food now sit.

I have worked for Ed for the past two years, and he is no stranger to stories about my adventures with Justin. When I first met him, he had just taken over from a previous administrator and I was approaching a week of vacation. Trying to get to know his new employees, Ed asked me what I had planned for my time off.

"I'm flying down to San Diego to spend the week with my best friend, Justin, to give his wife a break and help out."

"A break?" he asked, curious. "What are you helping out with exactly?

"They have three kids," I explained, "and Justin is in a wheel-chair."

"Like a manual wheelchair?"

"No, a power wheelchair. He can't use his hands or legs."

"So you're going down to take care of your friend and the three kids while his wife's away?"

"Yep."

He seemed intrigued, so I told him the whole story of Justin's disease. Over the next two years, he inquired frequently about Justin and became very familiar with our relationship.

When he sees me across the park, he makes eye contact and nods hello.

The smell of ribs and pulled pork rises from the grill. As I walk over to check the progress of the meat, I notice a young man in the distance in a wheelchair. It's been a little over a year since Justin first asked me about the trek through Spain. We've revisited the idea and talked about how it might come together, but the right time just hasn't revealed itself. Maybe there will never be a right time, just a right mind-set.

I look at the man in the wheelchair and think about my best friend. How often has Justin just pulled the trigger on what many would shy away from? Don't get me wrong—he isn't reckless; he plans out what needs to happen. But he's not the sort that focuses on how something will happen. He always starts with the *why*. If the *why* is strong enough, the *how* will come together.

Currently, Justin is 5,500 miles across the Atlantic Ocean in a medieval town in northwest Tuscany. He and Kirstin wanted their kids to experience the beautiful culture they'd embraced on their honeymoon many years before. So, while I'm at this picnic, Justin and his family are living in Lucca, Italy. It took them a year of planning, selling off possessions, working extra hours, and renting out their home to make it happen, but their *why* was important enough to make the sacrifice.

I walk to where my daughter is now pushing my son on the swings. Ed is standing close by, chatting with Becca, one of my good friends and coworkers. As their conversation comes to a close, I take the opportunity to bend Ed's ear.

"Ed, I have a quick question."

"Sure," he says, scanning the playground. "What's up?"

"I need six weeks off next summer," I say nonchalantly.

Ed's head snaps to attention. "All at once?" he asks.

"Yep!"

His eyes narrow. "That's going to be tough. What do you have planned?"

I begin to fill Ed in on the story behind the Camino de Santiago and Justin's desire to tackle the challenge this pilgrimage represents. As the words continue to come out of my mouth, I recognize the power that exists in speaking them out loud. Suddenly, this idea has a life it didn't have before. What was once simply an idea is now a possibility.

As Ed listens intently, his expression begins to turn from concern and apprehension to excitement and joy, and he nods his head as he processes his response.

When I finally stop talking, Ed looks me in the eye, and pointing his finger at my chest, says, "I will do everything in my power to get you the time off—on one condition."

"What's that?" I ask.

"Promise me you'll do everything in your power to document this journey on film."

Confused and a bit blindsided, I respond, "Okay . . . why?"

"Because," Ed states emphatically, "to not document it would be selfish and irresponsible! There's too much hope in this to not share it. The world needs to know hope like this exists!"

I didn't see that coming. I've been so focused on what this trip would mean to Justin and me, it never occurred to me it might mean something to anyone else. And yet the look on Ed's face speaks volumes.

Now where are we going to get a film crew?

As Ed turns his attention to his kids, I retreat to the picnic tables, sit down next to Donna, and take Olivia in my arms.

"I have the time off for Spain," I say.

Stunned, Donna replies, "What?"

"I just asked Ed for six weeks off next summer, and he agreed on the condition that we try to film the journey."

"That's crazy, but awesome!" Donna exclaims. "But why does he want you to film it?"

"He said we would be selfish and irresponsible if we didn't. He said there's too much hope in this to not share it." Then, laughing a little, I add, "He was pretty excited."

"Well," she says taking Olivia back, "you guys have waited long enough to do this. Sounds like you need to call Justin."

The next morning, Donna and I place a Skype call to Justin and Kirstin.

"Hey, you two," Donna opens the conversation. "How are things going?"

"You should see Justin on the cobblestone streets," Kirstin laughs.

Justin shakes his head and chuckles, "They're not very forgiving on my wheelchair. The 375 pounds of metal, rubber, plastic, and electronics vibrate so much I feel like dice in a Yahtzee cup."

"Are people getting used to seeing a guy in a power wheelchair yet?" I ask.

"At least they've finally stopped pointing and chattering in Italian about the crazy guy in the wheelchair," Kirstin says, laughing.

"Look at the bright side," I say. "You're definitely challenging their opinions about people with disabilities. You gotta love that!"

"Yeah," Justin says, smiling. "I do get a kick out of it. So, what's so important that we had to talk today?"

Donna gives my hand a gentle squeeze. I steal a quick glance at her and turn my attention back to Justin.

"Well," I say, fighting a smile, "when you get back, we need to start planning for Spain!"

He's clearly taken aback. I'm not sure what he was expecting, but this wasn't it.

"What do you mean?"

As I tell him about my conversation with Ed, I can almost

sense Justin's pulse racing through the Skype feed. By the time I get to the end, the smile on his face is a mile wide.

"He has only one condition," I continue.

"What's that?" Justin asks.

"Do you know anyone who might be interested in capturing this on film?"

AS READY AS WE'LL EVER BE

— JUSTIN —

WHEN WE ARRIVE BACK in the States, Patrick's words are still echoing in my head: *"Do you know anyone who might be interested in capturing this on film?"*

Amazingly enough, I think I might. Back in college, I knew a guy named Terry Parish, who is now the co-owner of a video agency in San Diego called emota, Inc. Documentaries aren't really their thing, but I figure it couldn't hurt to at least ask. So I give Terry a call, and after we get caught up on life, I give him a quick snapshot of what Patrick and I have in mind. Just like Ed, he's hooked immediately.

A few days later, I'm sitting across from Terry, his business partner, Chris Karcher, and several other members of the emota team in their conference room, telling them about Patrick, our past adventures, the progression of my disease, the Camino, and what we plan to do in the coming months. They are blown away by Patrick's response to my harebrained idea.

As the energy builds in the room, the excitement in their voices tells me all I need to know.

We've found our film crew.

But this is just the beginning. Because Patrick lives in Idaho and I live in California, planning and training for the Camino is going to be a challenge.

For years, Patrick and Donna have joked about how we need to move to Idaho. A recent trip up north was no exception. But this time, after three weeks with the Grays, both Kirstin and I feel a special stirring in our hearts. Even though winters in Idaho are cold and long, we can't shake the idea of moving. It doesn't make sense—Kirstin is a SoCal girl through and through, and after twenty-plus years in San Diego, I have become a convert to life in the sun—but it feels right. So we begin to pray.

Several weeks later, the pull toward Idaho has only become stronger, so after talking to our realtor, we Skype with Patrick and Donna.

After a few minutes of catching up, Kirstin nervously poses the question, "Are you sure you guys want us to move to Idaho?"

"Yes!" they exclaim simultaneously.

"Good," I break in, "because we're putting our house on the market tomorrow."

A mere four days later, we receive a full-price offer, and after several weeks of packing and paperwork, the Skeesucks are officially headed to Idaho.

Now the real preparations can begin.

| | |

As we get further into planning for this journey, other challenges begin to present themselves. Our travel expenses alone will be thousands of dollars. Not to mention all the equipment we're going to need: backpacks, shoes, rain gear, headlamps, sleeping bags, and some type of off-road wheelchair. Now that we're bringing along a film crew, the costs are mounting. But Patrick and I know we are supposed to do this, so we fight the temptation to get caught up in the *how* and keep moving forward.

Having studied dozens of topographical maps, read the blogs of many previous pilgrims, and watched numerous videos to get a feel for the terrain, we reach the obvious conclusion that a normal manual wheelchair will not be sufficient for this journey. If I'm going to make it from St. Jean Pied de Port to Santiago de Compostela, I'm going to need a chair that's lightweight enough for Patrick to push, yet strong enough to get me through three mountain passes and over hundreds of miles of cobblestone streets, rocky paths, gravel roads, and rugged terrain.

So, while Patrick starts his physical training, I hit the computer to set up a website to help us raise money for the trip. Using voice-automated software and my pen and tablet, I find that navigating my computer is difficult but not impossible. I'm grateful for the fingers I can still use.

After several hours of working on our website, I take a break to see if I can find a suitable wheelchair. Every morning, Patrick is at the gym before work; every night, he is either back at the gym or on the road riding his bike. But no matter how much he trains, there's no substitute for pushing a wheelchair for miles and days on end. We have to find something that will work.

It isn't long before I realize there are very few options, but soon I think I've discovered what we need—a lightweight, three-wheeled, off-road chair made out of aircraft aluminum, complete with mountain bike tires, disc brakes, and shocks. But it's eight thousand dollars.

We can't afford this.

Late in the evening, Patrick swings by my house after one of his workout sessions to get an update on my progress.

"So how's it coming?" he asks.

"Good," I tell him, nodding toward my computer screen. "Want to see our website?"

"Yeah, let's check it out."

As he leans in to get a closer look, I can see the sweat on his brow and smell the evidence of his hard work. It's only been a few months, and he is already getting lean. On any given day, he is up hours before me, and his head doesn't hit the pillow until well after mine.

"Just so you know," I laugh, "while you've been at the gym, I've been making it my goal to eat as much as possible."

"Very funny!" He shakes his head and chuckles. "So how much weight have you lost with your new diet?"

"Not sure, but all my clothes are fitting much looser."

"Nice work! Every pound will make a difference."

Turning back to my computer, I say, "Now check this out. I think I might have found a chair."

Using the stylus, I click the tab for the off-road chair.

"It looks like a three-wheeled baby jogger on steroids," Patrick says.

"Yeah, it does!"

Patrick puts his hand on my shoulder and says, "You've been busy. You've been eating super healthy, you've lost weight, the website you've been designing is complete, you created a Facebook page to help us raise awareness and hopefully some funds, *and* you've found us a chair!" Pointing to the computer screen, he asks, "So how much does this thing cost?"

"A lot!"

| | |

It's been several months since Patrick and I started preparing for the Camino. Since the launch of our website and Facebook page, many people have asked how they can help. Tonight, Patrick and I are sitting at a table outside Starbucks across from Josh Kinney, a mutual friend of ours from church. Josh and his wife, Kelli, are part owners of Bottle Cap Co., a business specializing in wholesaling bottle caps, and though I couldn't imagine a more unrelated business to sponsor our trip, they are ready to jump in and help make things happen.

"What is the one thing you guys need?" Josh asks.

Without hesitation, I reply, "A wheelchair!"

Patrick and I dive into the details about the chair I've found, why we think it is the one we need, and the time frame for having it built. When Josh asks how much it costs, I pull no punches: "Eight grand."

Josh sits back in his chair, takes a sip of his coffee, nods his head, and says, "Okay, I need to run this by our business partners."

Patrick and I thank him for even considering it. Eight thousand dollars is a lot to ask.

A few days later, my phone rings.

"Justin, it's Josh."

Bottle Cap Co. is all in.

After thanking Josh profusely, I call Patrick. "Guess what, Paddy—we've got our chair."

| | |

After measurements are taken of my legs, torso, and hips so the chair can be customized for my body, the countdown begins. The chair will take five months to build and is scheduled to arrive in March. With a departure date set for May 29, Patrick and I have only two months to train with it before we leave. I hope it's enough.

Patrick has been training on his own for weeks now, riding his bike and lifting weights twice a day, six days a week, in an effort to get stronger and increase his endurance. Unfortunately, all he has is a beat-up road bike that's over forty years old.

One night, as I'm putting some finishing touches on our website, my phone rings. It's Patrick, calling from work.

"Great news," he says. "We've got another donation! It's not cash, but it might be better!"

"What do you mean?"

"One of my coworkers, Dave, used to ride professionally, and he's got a ton of bikes. So, I'm in my office reading through some e-mails, and Dave pokes his head in my doorway and tells me to come outside. I follow him out to his car, and there's a beautiful, blue Bianchi road bike sitting there. I offered to buy it, but he just laughed at me and said, 'I don't have thousands of dollars to help sponsor you guys, but at least I can give you this.'"

"That's awesome!"

First Josh's company and now Dave—not to mention several thousand dollars of donations that have come in. Patrick and I are starting to feel a little overwhelmed by so much generosity.

| | |

Since getting his new bike, Patrick has been riding every chance he gets. Even now that the ground is covered in snow and the weather is much too cold to ride outside, he is keeping the twice-a-day routine going by riding on a trainer in his garage after his kids go to bed. Though he's quickly approaching the best shape of his life, we both know that until the chair arrives, we can't really know how ready he is.

While Patrick trains, I'm hard at work raising funds, generating buzz for the trip on social media, and filling in the gaps with a few design jobs to help pay the bills. Thanks to the limited mobility of my hands, everything I do on my computer takes much longer than it used to, but with everything Patrick is doing, I'm determined to keep at it. We catch a huge break when a friend suggests we create a gift registry at REI and post the link on our Facebook page. The response is overwhelming. In a matter of weeks, all the equipment Patrick and I need is sitting in his garage. Everything, that is, except my wheelchair.

Then, on a warm March afternoon, Patrick calls.

"Hey Skeez, Josh just pulled into my driveway with a large crate in the bed of his truck."

Kirstin, the kids, and I immediately head over to the Grays'.

As we roll into Patrick's driveway, he and Josh are tearing the crate apart. Patrick is so excited, he reminds me of the dad in *A Christmas Story* when his prized leg lamp finally arrives. Drills are whirring, packing peanuts are flying through the air, and screws are falling everywhere.

Once all the pieces are out of the crate, Patrick attaches the quick-release wheels to the body and adjusts the handlebars at the back of the chair to accommodate his height.

"Ready to go for a ride?" he asks.

I nod my head and smile. "I've never been more ready!"

I park my power wheelchair to the left of the off-road chair. Bending at the knees, Patrick slightly straddles my legs, slides his arms underneath mine, bear-hugs me, picks me up, rotates, and then sets me down on the padded seat of my new chariot. Little do we know, this is the first of hundreds of transfers that will take place over the course of the next three and a half months.

All six kids are eager to see this thing in action, so we take a stroll around the park across the street from the Grays' house. Each roll of the wheels feels exciting, and the sound of Patrick's footfalls behind me makes everything about this journey feel a little more real. Finally, we are ready to begin training, *together*! It feels so good to be moving as a unit. Like a couple of kids at Christmas, we are so giddy we take another lap. "You know," Patrick says, "this will be the first time you've let someone else control everything."

He's right. In my power wheelchair, I can determine when and where I go. I hadn't thought about this until now.

"Yeah," I say with a smile, "in this chair I'm completely at your mercy."

Though I intend it as a joke, Patrick takes it to heart. "That's a remarkable amount of trust to place in someone. I'm glad you've chosen me."

| | |

For the past six weeks, I've been with Patrick during his workouts. Though I have no control over where we go or how fast we get there, I am experiencing roads and trails that I'm not able to get to in my power chair. By giving up my freedom, I am gaining more of it, and I am finally beginning to appreciate what this trip is going to require—from both of us.

We've increased both the distance and the difficulty of the terrain we choose to tackle, with Patrick pushing me through the foothills of nearby Eagle, Idaho, where grades are as steep as 18 percent—which means an average rise of eighteen feet of elevation for every 100 feet of distance. The climbs are brutal on his legs, but each step brings new strength to his body and to both our wills. Patrick's relentless dedication to preparing his body to help me realize this dream is a powerful motivator for me. Though I can do little to prepare physically, I have continued to generate buzz via our Facebook page and website, trying to engage as many supporters as we can.

Every day while we train, new donations come in to sponsor our trip. Whether five dollars or five thousand, the questions of cost are slowly being answered, but what about the physical? Patrick has been training like a beast, but pushing me around the backcountry hills of Idaho is one thing. Propelling 250 pounds of dead weight over and across the Pyrenees is something else.

A number of people have offered to join us for the entire journey, but feeling cautious about who we would be spending so much time with, we've said, "No, thank you." But when Ted Hardy asks how he can help, it feels different. He's a good friend—and a firefighter. Patrick has known him for years and has traveled with him on several occasions.

Ted is a few years younger than we are, and he shares our zest for life and adventure. He thinks like us, has a similar sense of humor, and is as humble as they come. So when he approached us and said, "I feel like I'm supposed to help out in some way," we invited him to discuss it over dinner.

"We need help getting over the Pyrenees," Patrick tells him.

"If you came along, how long would you be able to stay?" I ask.

"I don't know. Maybe ten days?"

Patrick and I exchange a quick glance, and then he says what we're both thinking.

"You're coming to Spain."

| | |

With only a few weeks left before our departure, our training sessions are now up to twelve miles at a time, and Ted has joined us to get a feel for what he's signed up for.

On today's practice run, Patrick and Ted take turns pushing and pulling me up and down the steepest grades we can find. The process is simple, yet grueling. Whoever is pushing is harnessed in behind me, while the other guy is out front, pulling on a long red nylon strap attached to the sides of my elevated footrest by carabiners. The whole setup resembles an ox pulling a plow, with the farmer pushing from behind. The climbs are still difficult, but it is remarkable how much strain is alleviated by having another body to help.

Ten days before departure, we agree to train very little. Patrick, Ted, and I need to rest, but not before we tackle Quail Ridge. The final piece in our preparation puzzle, Quail Ridge is the steepest grade we can find. Kristin Armstrong, a local three-time Olympic gold medalist in the women's individual time trial in cycling, trains on this ascent, and more than a few local vehicles have had difficulties chugging up the steep road. With sections as steep as 25 percent, it's the only hill that will come close to what we will face in the Pyrenees. If we can climb Quail Ridge, we're as ready as we'll ever be.

While Patrick transfers me from my power chair to my off-road chair and wraps our makeshift harness around his waist, Ted grabs the reins in front. Slowly, step-by-step, we begin the ascent. The concrete below us is a poor substitute for the trail we will face, but the grade is still punishing. The climb is a little over a mile, and only a quarter mile in, Patrick and Ted are both hurting.

"This is much more difficult than the hill from a few days ago," Patrick wheezes. "And we haven't even hit the steepest section yet."

While Patrick and Ted push and pull the chair forward, I lean from side to side to counter the slopes of driveways, and I can already feel some fatigue in my core muscles.

As the road bends left and right, Patrick has to put so much leverage into pushing that his arms and face are nearly parallel to the ground, and he has to rely on Ted and me to tell him where to go. Sensing that Patrick could use a break, Ted shouts out from the front, "Let's switch!"

Patrick locks the brakes, but because the hill is so steep, he refuses to move until Ted has unharnessed himself and made his way to the back of the chair. As Patrick moves to the side and allows Ted to grab the handles and lean his body into the chair, I feel myself inch backward before Ted puts even more of his weight into it. We all exchange knowing glances.

What are we getting ourselves into?

As Patrick wraps the waist harness around Ted and secures him to my wheelchair, Ted smiles and says, half-jokingly, "If Justin gets away from us, at least he'll have an anchor to slow him down."

We all laugh, but we're a little nervous at the prospect of the chair cascading down the hill with me in it and one of them skipping behind me like a rock across a pond. Suppressing our nerves, we continue the climb. After a few hundred feet, Ted shouts, "It feels like I'm walking in wet concrete."

"I know!" Patrick yells back. "My shoes feel heavier with every step." Ignoring the burning in their thighs, calves, and lungs, they keep moving me forward.

After a grueling hour and fifteen minutes, we finally reach the top and take a moment to rest. Ted is on a tight timeline and has just a few minutes left before he has to get back to work, so as soon as he and Patrick catch their breath, we begin the descent.

This time, Patrick is pulling back on the handlebars, as a counterweight to my chair, and Ted is strapped in eight feet behind him, pulling back on the red nylon harness, which is now attached to the back of the wheelchair. The hill is so steep, the chair wants to lurch forward with every step. With both guys now behind me, I'm staring straight downhill, hoping the straps and carabiners are secure enough to hold me.

After we pass the steepest section, Ted says the words we've been dreading.

"Sorry, guys, but I gotta get back to the station."

Unharnessing himself, he turns to Patrick, and before dashing off to his car, says, "Don't worry. You've got this."

The combination of fatigue and the steep grade are giving Patrick's body a taste of what the Camino will be like when we're on our own. It takes everything he has to complete the last quarter mile as he leans back, taking short steps to prevent the chair from gaining any momentum. As he bears the full weight of the load, straining to keep the chair from lurching down the hill, I begin to feel the magnitude of what I'm asking of my friend.

What are we doing? What if this is too much?

With the bottom of the hill in sight, I shout out a few words of encouragement.

"Nice work! You got this!"

When we get to the bottom, Patrick staggers to the van to get my power chair. When he transfers me from one chair to the other, I can feel the moisture from his saturated shirt. He is completely soaked and looks exhausted.

"So, what do you think?" I ask him. "Are we ready?"

"As ready as we'll ever be."

6
DEPARTURE

— PATRICK —

A YEAR OF PREPARATION has led us to this moment.

I have never been away from my wife and kids for more than a week, but now I'm going to be gone for a month and a half. Though I'm excited, I'm also anxious about leaving Donna and the kids behind. Our one-stop flight from Boise to Paris is due to leave in an hour, and Justin and I are looking at nearly six weeks before we meet up with our wives in Santiago de Compostela. It seems like an eternity from now.

Surrounded by our families, we sense the uneasiness in our wives, children, and parents. We pause for a moment of prayer—for traveling mercies, safety, and wisdom. Many hugs are exchanged before we begin to work our way toward the security gate. After saying good-bye to my parents, I hug Kirstin and the Skeesuck kids while my family hugs Justin.

"I'll take care of him," I hear Justin say to Donna. "I'll keep him safe."

"I know you will," she says with a smile.

As we approach security, all three of my kids are in tears,

but Cambria is crying the hardest. I bend down so our foreheads touch and place my hands gently on the sides of her face.

"I love you so much!"

"Please don't go," she chokes out between sobs.

"I'll be back in six weeks," I reassure her. "We'll Skype, and you can follow the updates on Facebook."

"But I don't want you to go," she whispers as I hug her again.

"I know," I tell her as tears fill my eyes.

The rest of my family joins us, and we become one mass of emotion.

Donna chokes out a final good-bye, followed by, "I love you so much!"

"I love you, too!"

Nearby, Justin's older brother, Ryan, stands at his side, tears of pride and joy streaming down his face. The Skeesuck children then hug Justin again. Lauren's face is wet, and Kirstin wipes tears from her eyes as she gives Justin one final kiss.

As we work our way through security, Justin's three-wheeled-baby-jogger-on-steroids draws plenty of stares. Earlier, at the ticket counter, a young woman had said, "That's quite the wheelchair. What are you guys planning on doing in Paris?"

When we told her, she just stared at us, mouth open.

Now, the TSA agent says, "I've never seen one like this," pointing at Justin's chair. "What are you planning on doing, climbing a mountain?"

"Kind of," Justin replies, smiling.

The TSA agent tilts his head forward and raises his eyebrows. "Seriously?"

At the gate, a bright, peppy attendant puts a tag on Justin's chair so we can check it.

"Why do you need a chair like this for Paris?" she asks.

When we tell her, her eyes pop open like a deer in the headlights. "Holy—" she begins before catching herself.

"You'd think they'd never heard of anyone hiking five hundred miles through mountains in a wheelchair," Justin kids as we head toward the Jetway.

At the door of the plane, I transfer Justin into a waiting aisle chair (a small, skinny wheelchair used to assist those who have difficulty getting on and off planes). Once he is strapped into the aisle chair, I pull the quick-release pins to collapse the handlebars of the off-road chair and shorten the leg rest. After the process is complete, the chair is a good foot shorter, both in length and height. The ground crew takes the chair for stowage, while I grab Justin's seat cushion and join him on the plane.

After putting our backpacks and Justin's cushion into the overhead compartments, I lift Justin to transfer him to his seat. In smaller planes, like this one, I have to be careful so I don't hit my head. The narrow aisle and minimal space between the rows of seats mean I also have to be incredibly mindful of my feet and body while I lift him.

The whole boarding process, from start to finish, takes about ten minutes.

A few hours later, we land in San Francisco for our layover, and I reverse the process. After unloading our luggage and waiting for the aisle chair, I transfer Justin, wheel him off the plane, secure the leg rests and handlebars on the off-road chair, transfer Justin again, and wait for the next plane. Then I push him down the Jetway and repeat the entire process.

It's not until we're on the plane to Paris that I can finally relax a little bit. Justin and I have traveled together so much that most of this has become automatic. Still, because of all the moving pieces, I'm always a little nervous until we're settled on the plane to our final destination. The more connecting flights we have, the greater the likelihood that something on his chair will get broken or that something will accidentally be left behind.

The eleven-hour flight to Paris offers plenty of time to rest. We listen to music, watch a movie, and try to sleep, but sleep eludes us. There's so much excitement and anticipation.

"We're actually doing this!" Justin says.

"I know. It's kind of hard to believe."

He pauses for a second, then asks, "How are you feeling? Scared? Worried?"

"Actually, I'm not sure what I'm feeling."

After I put Justin's headphones over his ears and help him find a movie to watch, I turn to the screen on the seatback in front of me. I'm scrolling through the many options, but the titles don't even register. My mind is still in the Boise airport.

| | |

The first time I ever laid eyes on Donna was my very first day at Northwest Nazarene College. She was playing a game as a part of freshman orientation, and when we made eye contact, she smiled so big, the corners of her eyes curled up. It was the first time I had ever seen someone's eyes smile.

A few days later, I asked her out.

Much of our first date was spent sitting on a bench in front of the campus library.

"So what are you planning to study?" I asked.

"I'm going to be a teacher."

"Really," I said, inching a little closer to her. "Both my parents are teachers. What makes you want to do that?"

She shook her head and said, "I don't know. I've just always known it's what I'm supposed to do. How about you?"

"I'm looking at a degree in biology, but I really don't know yet."

We continued to talk for hours, and when I walked her back to her dorm, I reached for her hand just as she reached for mine. When I kissed her good night, I opened my eyes to find her looking right at me, her eyes smiling the same way they had a few days before. I fell fast. And hard.

Donna and I dated throughout college, and our courtship led to the obvious question. I had it planned out perfectly. After a day spent hiking in the Wallowa Mountains, we were headed back down the trail. I knelt down on one knee in the middle of a small footbridge. The gaps in the boards were an inch wide, and I could see the rushing water of the river below. As I proposed, all I could think was: *Don't drop the ring! Don't drop the ring!*

Thankfully, I didn't, and she said yes!

The wedding was set for June 28, 1997. Naturally, Justin was my best man.

Surrounded by family and friends, we married, and I remember feeling overjoyed while also thinking, *Don't screw this up!* After honeymooning on Vancouver Island in British Columbia, Donna and I settled in the Seattle area to begin our life together. When my biology degree proved less than marketable, we moved to Vancouver, Washington, and I went to work loading freight onto trucks while Donna looked for a job that would utilize her degree in elementary education.

Donna subbed for a year before I decided it was time for me to return to college. We moved back to Idaho, and I enrolled at

Northwest Nazarene again to pursue a degree in secondary education while Donna found a teaching job. After graduating with a second bachelor's degree, I taught high school for a few years, but it wasn't a good fit. So I went back to school for a third round, this time to get a nursing degree.

After graduating, I worked at the bedside for several years, the majority of which were spent in orthopedics. Eventually, I was asked to apply for a position at an area hospital to manage their spine program. Always up for a challenge, I applied, got the job, and began navigating the task of keeping both the hospital and the surgeons I worked for happy. I tracked patient outcomes, dealt with physician and patient complaints, researched best practices, developed financial projections for new clinics, and expanded the program.

Four years, two promotions, and countless seventy-hour weeks later, I'm overworked, overstressed, disengaged from my wife and kids, and now I'm flying across the ocean and leaving them all for six weeks.

What am I doing?

| | |

After three more movies, a couple of meals, and hours of music, I feel my eyelids finally begin to droop—just as the wheels touch the runway in Paris.

Our film crew—Terry from emota, and Mike, who joined the ranks two weeks ago—are on the same flight. Once we're all off the plane, the four of us make our way to the railway station to catch a train to the city of Bayonne, in the southwest corner of France. There we'll spend a few days resting and acclimating to a new schedule before we begin our pilgrimage.

Once our tickets are squared away, we work with the information desk to ensure that a lift or ramp is available so Justin can get on the train. After multiple assurances that everything has been taken care of, we sit and wait. The train platforms are one level below us, so we find a bench where I can sit next to Justin and rest.

As the time nears for our train to arrive, we hustle to the elevator with one backpack on Justin's chair and mine on my back. The elevator takes forever to descend to the platform level, and when the bell finally dings to announce our arrival, our train is already in the station.

"Where's the ramp?" I ask, searching the area.

"I don't know," says Justin. "There's no lift, either."

With less than a minute until departure, Terry and Mike load their gear onto the train and board while I frantically look for someone to help us.

Seconds later, the doors close and the train pulls away, taking Mike and Terry with it. Standing on the platform, all I can do is wave good-bye.

"Well, that sucks," I exclaim, shaking my head and laughing.

Justin just smiles and says, "Let's head back upstairs. See if we can figure something out."

Back at the information desk, we explain our plight, and one of the clerks takes it upon herself to become our personal advocate. She transfers our tickets to the next—and last—train to Bayonne and assures us that she will personally make all of the necessary arrangements for accessibility. Once again, we sit and wait. When we ride the painfully slow elevator back down to the platform, the help we need is available. Minutes later, we are on the train to Bayonne.

Our cabin is surprisingly empty. With brakes locked and wheelchair secured, I plop onto a seat across from Justin as he leans back in his wheelchair.

"How long till we get to Bayonne?" Justin asks, stifling a yawn.

"About six hours."

"Well, it's definitely been an interesting first day," he jokes.

I have to admit, the whole situation seems surreal—just the two of us in a foreign country with only a wheelchair and two backpacks. Normally, Justin travels with a bedside commode, a shower chair, and a number of other medical supplies, but given that we have to carry everything with us on the Camino, we decided to do it bare bones, so we've brought only the essentials. Together, our backpacks weigh about thirty pounds. Each one contains a sleeping bag, three pairs of antimicrobial underwear, three pairs of socks, one pair of shorts, one pair of pants that convert into shorts, two T-shirts, two long-sleeve shirts, a jacket, a stocking cap, and a rain parka. We also have flip-flops, the shoes on our feet, our guidebook, headlamps, a small tool kit for the wheelchair, insulated chaps for Justin's legs, and a collapsible urinal.

Shortly after making the decision to scale back on our equipment, we had notified Chris and Terry on a video call to emota. They were excited at the prospect of a more challenging journey, but they also told us that funding for the documentary was looking grim. Well short of our financial target, Terry and Chris asked if we could delay the journey for a year.

"No!" I said, shaking my head emphatically. "We have no guarantee how much time Justin has. We're going this year, with or without a film crew."

After the call ended, I looked at Justin and said, "I hope I didn't speak out of turn there."

"You didn't," he assured me.

"How much time *do* you think you have?" I asked, not really wanting to hear the answer.

Justin just sighed and said, "I have no idea. But I don't see this happening if I get any worse . . . and I *am* going to get worse. It's just a question of when."

| | |

Mortality has a way of changing your perspective. That's something we both came to grips with well before Justin's health started to decline.

When we were in grade school, my mom became ill during a camping trip. At first, the illness presented much like a stomach bug—nausea, vomiting, diarrhea, and extreme fatigue. But one night something changed, and my dad rushed her to the hospital. The doctors diagnosed her with toxic shock syndrome—a severe bacterial infection that had invaded her body and quickly escalated to a life-threatening level. They told my father that if he had waited much longer to take her to the hospital, she would have died that night in bed.

I'll never forget seeing her in the hospital bed with an IV in each arm, looking so drawn and fragile. The doctors were so concerned about her dehydration that the IV fluids flowed more than they dripped. Mom spent three days in the ICU and eight more in the medical unit before she was finally able to come home.

For years afterward, I was frightened by how close my mother had come to death, to the point where my fear of losing her bordered on paranoia. I remember one day I came home from school, and our car was in the driveway, but there was no one in the house. I became hysterical before finding her in the backyard pulling weeds.

With time, though, my fear helped shape a new perspective. Almost losing my mom taught me that life is short and time is precious. We need to make the most of what we have.

A few years later, Justin's mother was diagnosed with an aggressive form of breast cancer. Fortunately, chemotherapy and a mastectomy saved her life, but like me, Justin quickly learned not to take a single moment for granted.

After watching our mothers face death, and now seeing my best friend doing the same, I've begun to wonder: *What if I died right now? Would I wish I had lived my life differently, or would I be proud of where I am when my light burns out?*

| | |

As midnight draws near and the train finally approaches Bayonne, Justin and I are on the verge of delirium. We haven't slept for thirty-five hours.

We find Terry and Mike waiting for us at the station, and together we stagger a mile through the darkened streets to our hotel. I'm beyond exhausted, and Justin is desperate for any semblance of a bed. After checking in, we make our way to the elevator that will take us up to the fourth floor, only to discover that it is just three feet wide by three feet deep.

After transferring Justin onto a bench in the hotel lobby, I try to break down the chair to make it fit, but it quickly becomes clear that there is no way we are going to get it into the elevator.

Spent and defeated, I sit down next to Justin. Just across from us, the girl at the counter, who has been watching the drama unfold, begins to apologize about the situation. I'm so tired, I can barely follow her French.

As she's talking, Justin looks past her and sees an office chair on wheels. "Can we use your office chair?" he asks.

"Oui!" she says graciously.

I retrieve the makeshift wheelchair and position it beside the bench where Justin is sitting. I can see the exhaustion in his eyes, and I'm running on empty myself.

With shoulders slouched and moving almost in slow motion, I find the strength to pick up Justin and set him down on the office chair. We lock his off-road wheelchair in a room on the main floor and get into the elevator—one of those old ones with a gate you close after entering. Because Justin can't use his hands, I have to ride with him. Nine square feet doesn't leave much room for two full-grown men, two backpacks, and an office chair. As I back Justin into the elevator and squeeze in next to him, I realize that his face is right at my belt level. After thirty-six sleepless hours on the road, neither of us is the epitome of great personal hygiene, but he definitely drew the short straw.

"Dude, you stink!" he says, crinkling his nose.

"Yeah, I know," I concede. "I can smell me too."

After what feels like an eternity, the elevator squeaks and grinds its way to the fourth floor, and we get out. As I pull Justin out into the hall, the chair wheels catch on the thick carpet, which is buckled from years of use. As the chair spins, Justin starts to teeter, and I have to grab his shoulders to keep him from falling onto the floor.

Naturally, our room is the next-to-last room down the hall and around the corner from the elevator. Slowly and carefully, I push and pull the office chair down the hall. At times, I'm facing Justin and can't see where we're going, so he has to look back over his shoulder to give me directions. We finally make it to the corner and turn left. Thirty more feet and a few more close calls caused by wrinkles in the carpet, and we are finally at our door.

Bleary-eyed, I fumble for the key and open our room. As the hinges squeak and the door swings open, we are greeted by a six-inch step immediately inside the door.

"A step? Really?" Justin says.

We both hang our heads and begin to laugh—and the volume soon grows, fueled by a lack of sleep and a little anger.

"Shhhh, you're going to wake the neighbors," Justin says to me through tears.

"*I'm* going to wake the neighbors?"

Anxious to bring this day to a close, I grab the desk chair from the corner of the room and set it next to the step. I then back Justin into the entryway until he is as close as possible to the step, and for the twelfth time since we left Boise, I transfer him from one chair to another. As I drag the desk chair over to the edge of the bed, the legs catch against the carpet.

"Okay, end of the line," I say. Reaching over Justin, I pull back the covers and then lift him into bed.

"Good night, Skeez."

"Good night, Paddy."

My mind and body are beyond exhaustion. I have never trans-ferred Justin this much in such a short period of time. My shoulders and back throb with a deep aching pain, and my head feels like it weighs a hundred pounds. After calling my wife to let her know we made it, all I want to do is sleep. But my soul feels differ-ent. Sitting on the edge of the bed listening to Justin's deep, slow breathing, I can't help but appreciate his willingness to be here, his desire to take life by the horns and truly live.

Lying in bed, eyes staring toward a ceiling hidden by darkness, I am amazed how Justin faces life lived in a wheelchair. In spite of having more physical challenges than anyone I know, he has lived more than most. Nothing seems to hold him back.

So what's holding me back? What's keeping me from living life the same way?

— PART III —

CAMINO DE SANTIAGO

7

I WONDER IF . . .

— PATRICK —

ON JUNE 2, our final morning in Bayonne, we hear that a storm has settled over the Pyrenees Mountains and it has been raining there for the past few days. At the railway station, the woman at the ticket counter tells us that the train from Bayonne to our starting point in St. Jean Pied de Port has been shut down due to a mudslide that washed out the tracks. Either we find an alternate means of transportation for the thirty-five-mile trip, or we're not getting there today.

A number of buses are headed that way, but none with a lift to get Justin and his chair aboard. Already we're finding that accessibility in Europe leaves much to be desired. Terry and Mike go on ahead while we attempt to hire an accessible vehicle, but the language barrier makes communication difficult. My French is pathetic at best, and Justin's Spanish is of no use here. After much discussion with the folks at the train station, we are mildly certain that a taxi is on the way.

We wait for an hour, and when our ride finally arrives, it is the smallest "accessible" vehicle I have ever seen—sort of a hunchbacked version of a Mini Cooper. And when the driver steps out from the car, the picture is complete. He has the wild hair of a mad professor, with clothes that are disheveled and stained, but he is all joy and smiles. While he lowers the ramp on the back of the car, he assures us that Justin and the chair will fit just fine, as long as Justin leans to one side and tilts his head. Even so, the fit is incredibly tight, and I have to climb into the car and reach over the backseat to guide the chair in. With the footrest pushed all the way in, Justin and his wheelchair are still about two inches from fitting.

With one final heave, the Frenchman shoves Justin further into the car while at the same time the loudest explosion of gas that Justin and I have ever heard escapes the cabdriver's body.

We all begin to laugh, and he says with a thick French accent, "Oh, I made an unfortunate sound!"

Pleased with his joke, he flashes us two thumbs up, slides behind the wheel, and starts the engine. Finally, we're on our way to St. Jean to meet up with Ted and the film crew, with "Lovesong," by The Cure, blaring from the speakers.

— JUSTIN —

After an hour-long ride wedged in the back of the taxi, I have a pretty good idea of what it's like to be a sardine. And though I can't stand up and stretch when we reach our destination, it feels good to at least be able to shift my position and begin to work out the stiffness in my neck.

At the hotel, the elevator is too small again, so we borrow a standard wheelchair and leave mine locked in a downstairs closet. As we settle into our tiny room, we're joined by Terry and Mike—and now Ted, who recently arrived in town. With two twin beds and five people crowding in, there's little room to spare, so the four other guys sit down on the beds and I'm in the borrowed wheelchair just inside the door. I miss the size and accessibility of American hotel rooms.

Terry and Mike have decided that a two-man crew is not enough for the challenges of filming our journey. Yesterday, Mike made a few calls, and now he tells us that two new members of the team are on their way to St. Jean.

This represents a real commitment on the part of emota, who had told us shortly before we left the States that they would foot the bill for filming our journey, even though funds were tight. But Terry and Chris hadn't planned on adding people to the crew.

A few minutes later, we hear a knock on the door. When Patrick opens it, a tall, lean young man with long brown hair, bright blue eyes, and a perfect smile—the spitting image of Zac Efron—is standing there.

"Hi, who are you?" I ask.

"I'm Jasper. I'm one of your videographers."

As Jasper squeezes into the room, he says, "Mike called me yesterday as I was headed up to Mount Hood to do some skiing. He said he needed some help on an amazing project in Spain."

"When he said he was interested," Mike chimes in, "I said, 'Great, can you be here in twenty-four hours?'"

"So, do you know why you're here?" I ask.

"Not exactly, but here I am! So tell me what we're up to."

As we head out to explore the town of St. Jean, Patrick and I fill Jasper in on how the whole adventure started, and we can see that he's excited. He and Mike previously worked together on some ski film projects, where Jasper gained experience with filming action footage.

When we return to the hotel, we leave Jasper to familiarize himself with the more than one hundred pounds of video gear Terry has assembled while we go to a nearby bar to pick up some snacks for tomorrow's hike.

As we're about to leave the bar, I hear an unfamiliar voice call out in a thick French accent, "Are you Justeen?"

A short, wiry, black-haired young man with a thin, wispy mustache is smiling at us.

"I am Robeen. I'm your driver!"

A native of Bosnia, Robin skis professionally and was part of a film Mike worked on. In addition to his skills as a production assistant and driver, Robin brings fluency in Spanish, French, and Bosnian to the team.

As afternoon turns to evening, the members of our newly expanded team—the four-man film crew along with Ted, Patrick, and me—gather around several tables at a local café. Our excitement builds as Terry and Mike explain the gear they've brought along and the logistics of filming out on the trail.

With the sun dropping behind the Pyrenees to the west, we enjoy cold beers and a hearty meal while we lay out our expectations of the film crew.

Patrick looks at each one and says, "You guys are here to film, to capture what unfolds. But you can't help us in any way. We want things to happen the way they would have if you guys weren't here filming. So, you're just flies on the wall—with cameras."

As the conversation comes to a close, we pay our tab and head back to the hotel, where we settle in for as good a sleep as you can get the night before you take on the Camino with a wheelchair.

| | |

— PATRICK —

In the morning, as we're packing up to leave, I can't find my glasses anywhere. After I thoroughly search the room, Justin asks, "Did you leave them at the café?"

Crap!

Going back to get them is not an option. The restaurant won't reopen for several hours, and we need to get moving if we want to achieve our first day's objective of reaching the town of Roncesvalles (seventeen miles of mountainous terrain away) in time for dinner.

Outside, we are greeted by bright sunshine—after several days of unrelenting rain—with only a scattering of clouds to soften the depths of the cerulean sky.

Justin, Ted, and I meet the rest of the team at a small café down the street from our hotel. The smell of fresh baguettes fills the air, and the aroma of rich French coffee floods our senses— we can almost taste it. After purchasing some of the fresh bread and coffee, we make sandwiches with cured ham and cheese while the film crew preps their gear. Feeling well-fueled for the morning of exertion we are about to face, we get up to leave.

As we're gathering our things, our server approaches, points to the cameras, and asks what we're doing.

"We're walking the Camino," Ted says.

"In *that*?" she asks, pointing to Justin's chair.

Ted nods and says, *"Oui."*

The woman laughs and begins to walk away. As she turns, shaking her head, we can hear her say in a thick French accent, "No, you're not."

This woman isn't the first person to point out that the odds are against us. Just yesterday, in fact, when we went to the Pilgrim's Office in St. Jean to register for the Camino and purchase our pilgrim's passports (*credenciales del peregrino*), everyone we talked to just shook their heads and told us we would never make it through the Pyrenees with a wheelchair. We heard the same word—*impassable*—a lot.

By now, Justin and I have become accustomed to negativity and doubt. Many of our friends and family members are concerned about our safety on this journey, but several told us we were completely stupid to even attempt it. Discouraging as it may be, it is fuel for our fire.

"We will make it to Santiago even if you have to strap me to a donkey," Justin says.

Leaving the woman's pessimism behind us, we begin our pilgrimage—and right out of the gate we're struggling. A steeply ascending country road requires Ted to strap in and pull much earlier than we had anticipated, and soon we are on an even steeper dirt trail littered with brick-size rocks.

Back in Idaho, the trails and roads we trained on were flat from side to side. Here, every turn has us on a lateral pitch that forces Justin to counterbalance by leaning his weight in the opposite direction. The thousands of images and videos we culled through in preparation for the Camino have failed to give us a true appreciation for what we are now facing.

As we struggle onward and upward, the camera crew runs ahead to capture shots at the best angle. They are working every bit as hard as we are, but with our focus on the task at hand, we soon forget they're here.

Though we stop every half mile or so to eat a protein bar and drink some water, by three miles into this seventeen-mile day, I am on the verge of retching from exhaustion. The air is cooler and drier than we expected, but still my body is lathered with sweat. All I can do is rehydrate and pound down another protein bar. We have to keep moving.

Ted and I begin to switch positions even more frequently. Pushing and pulling use different muscles, but already all of those muscles are becoming fatigued.

After several hours at near maximum exertion, we find a place where the ground is somewhat level and stop to rest. As we catch our breath and drink more water, a fellow pilgrim approaches us. Introducing himself as Father Kevin, an Episcopalian priest, he asks if he can say a blessing over our travels. We welcome the offer and close our eyes as he prays over each one of us a blessing of safety, guidance, and provision. For me, it's validation, acknowledgment that we are on the right path.

— JUSTIN —

Reinvigorated, we continue to work toward our designated lunch stop, Refuge Orisson, one of the pilgrim-specific hostels known as *albergues* that can be found in cities and villages along the Camino route.

The trail has been incredibly difficult up to this point. Patrick and Ted are constantly slipping on the rocks and loose shale as they work to propel the 250 pounds of my fully loaded wheelchair uphill. But now we're on a section of paved road, a brief reprieve from the rugged path that has been jarring my bones for the past several hours. I feel like I've been riding a bike down an old washboard road.

Not long into this next stretch of the Camino, we meet a young British woman named Lucy, who lives in Austria. Her curiosity about the cameras accompanying us has gotten the better of her, and she asks what we're doing on the Camino. We tell her our story and ask about hers. Her life is full of questions—about faith, family, and a potential career change.

"So, what's your job?" Ted asks.

"I'm an opera singer."

"You have to sing for us then," I say with a smile.

Lucy gives us a choice. "Would you rather hear an operatic piece or an old English folk song?"

We choose the folk song. As she begins to sing, the sound of the wind at our backs, eagles crying in the distance, and the far-off jingling of bells around the necks of the sheep on the hillsides offer the perfect accompaniment to her extraordinary a cappella performance. The intense colors of the landscape and the purity of Lucy's voice bring each of us to silent tears of appreciation. It is a moment of pure beauty.

When she finishes, I say to her, "So you're an opera singer. What's your new career going to be?"

"I'm an accompanist; I want to be a soloist."

Here in the heart of the Pyrenees, we've been blessed to witness her first public solo.

Having set a pace that is quicker than ours, Lucy moves on ahead and gradually fades in the distance, but the beauty of her voice has filled us with renewed energy. Despite the strain on Patrick and Ted, and the fatigue in my core muscles from the constant pitching from side to side, we keep trudging slowly up the long hill to a stone cross surrounded by a simple fence, which serves as a shrine to the many pilgrims who come this way.

The climb has been punishing on all of us, and far more strenuous for me than I had imagined. My back and neck are tight and feel misaligned, and as we reach a plateau and stop to rest, I shift in my wheelchair to take the pressure off the sore spots on my backside. The chair has shocks intended to mitigate the jarring nature of the path, but they have proved no match for the rocks, large tufts of grass, and grooves in the trail from more than a thousand years of use. In spite of all this, Patrick and I smile at each other in silent understanding. There's no place we'd rather be.

After stretching his calves to work out the built-up tension, Patrick sits down on the side of the path and reclines in the damp grass.

"Listen to that," he says. "Nothing but silence. . . . It's a beautiful sound."

Embracing the quiet, I look back at the distant green hills below, where we started the day. It's difficult to process how far we've come.

As we get ready to move on, I turn my attention to the pathway ahead of us.

"That can't be the trail!" I say in utter disbelief

In the distance, the hillside is littered with irregular stones and haphazard steps of earth and rock—as if a staircase collapsed and was covered by dirt and shattered boulders. There's no way we're getting through this with me in my chair.

The word *impassable* is echoing in our minds. We are beginning to appreciate what the people at the Pilgrim's Office meant. Maybe they were right.

Nevertheless, Ted straps in and begins to pull the makeshift red nylon harness attached by carabiners to the leg rest on my wheelchair. With Patrick pushing from behind, we gradually make our way closer to the base of the obstacle-ridden path. The closer we get, the more obvious it becomes that no amount of pushing and pulling is going to get me up this next stretch of trail.

Patrick and Ted chock the wheels with rocks to keep the chair from rolling down the steep path while they look for an alternate route. Leaving their backpacks on the ground nearby, they take a scouting run up the hillside about a hundred yards. By the time they return, they've agreed that the only option is to carry me through the debris.

As we discuss the best way to handle the carry, Patrick tells us, "There's also some good news. I went a little farther up the trail, and around the bend at the top of the hill there's pavement."

Filled with the hope of some relief from the rough path, we are motivated to keep moving. With the brakes secured and the wheelchair anchored, Ted and Patrick retrieve a nylon sling we've brought along for such an occasion. As they gently slide the fabric underneath me, I psych myself up for this next challenge, and my two friends ready themselves to lift me out of my seat.

"On three!" says Ted. "One, two, three!"

The four nylon handles, two on each side of the sling, are suddenly drawn taut as gravity enforces its inexorable law. Ted and Patrick struggle to keep their backs straight as they lift me out of the chair and begin to carefully navigate the rough and steep terrain.

Progress is painfully slow. After only fifteen feet, they have to lay me down on the ground and rest for a minute

Three hundred feet . . . fifteen feet at a time . . . how long is this going to take?

"Let's keep moving," Patrick says as he grabs the straps of my sling again.

As he and Ted carry me, I'm in a reclined position and completely at their mercy. Step-by-step, they work their way forward, maneuvering over randomly placed stones while trying to keep their balance—and not drop me—on the uneven terrain. We make it another fifteen feet before fatigue forces us to stop and rest a second time. Three more carries and we are almost halfway.

My friends lay me down in a patch of grass while they scout ahead to determine the best route. Closing my eyes, I just listen, taking in this moment of reprieve. All I can hear are the bells around the necks of far-off livestock and the distant cry of a hawk. The wind whispers its way through the grass around me, and these few short minutes seem to last for hours. As I lie here, questioning how much more of this my body can take and whether it will be enough to last this monthlong pilgrimage, I sense someone approaching me.

When I open my eyes, I see an elderly Basque man straddling me, wearing faded jeans, a yellow plaid shirt, and a black beret; I am captivated by his huge smile. Before I can say anything, he bends down and slaps my face. It isn't a hard slap—more like the affectionate slap an Italian mother might give her son to let him know how much she cares—but coming from a complete stranger, it's more than a little unexpected.

"Incroyable!" he says to me in French.

When I respond in Spanish—*"¿Cómo estás?"*—he switches languages.

"¡Bien!"

"¡Estoy muy loco!" I say with a laugh. I can tell he thinks we're crazy.

"Estar un poco mal de la cabeza es algo bueno."

He's taxing my limited Spanish, but I think he just said that being crazy in the head can be a good thing.

As we continue to converse, Robin offers to translate.

"He says he's spent the last twelve years tending sheep in these mountains and maintaining a small refuge hut a little farther up the hill for pilgrims caught in inclement weather. In all that time, he has never seen a man in a wheelchair come over the Pyrenees."

With a look of approval, the man points at Patrick and Ted and says, *"Muy fuerte."* Flashing a thumbs-up sign, he adds, *"Bueno, muy bueno,"* and continues up the hillside toward a hut made of earth and stone.

Halfway up the hill, the man stops and turns back toward us. Raising his arms with fists clenched, he shouts, *"¡Lo imposible es posible!"*

Such a brief interaction . . . but there is so much power in his words. They wash over us and fill us with a strength grounded in the idea that things are only impossible because they haven't been done yet.

With this renewed strength, my friends pick me up again and we finish the long, slow march to the top. After a quick water break, they head back down the trail to retrieve my wheelchair while I enjoy another few moments of solitude, lying in the grass and embracing another moment to rest.

When the guys return with my chair and load me into it, we're ready for the next section of trail. The path is now smooth, and the thought of getting onto a paved surface fills us with hope. But as we travel around the bend to the left, we recognize the trail for what it really is.

"That's not pavement," shouts Ted. "It's mud!"

What Patrick, with his poor vision, could have sworn was asphalt was instead more than a hundred yards of thick, black mud. With the mountain sloping up to the left and a cliff dropping hundreds of feet to our right, our only option is to go through the muck.

Though no one will say it out loud, we all have the same thought racing through our minds: *This is just the first day! How in the world are we going to make this happen?*

Pushing the unknown future aside, we keep moving, one foot in front of the other and one turn of the wheel at a time. Ted and Patrick take turns, one donning the harness and pulling like an ox while the other pushes the chair from behind. The sweat pouring down their faces stings their eyes, and the sweat running down their arms makes it difficult to grip the handlebar at the back of the wheelchair. With every muscle screaming for a break, lungs burning for more oxygen, and bodies desperate for another drink, they push slowly onward to the end of this stretch of incredible resistance.

The physical strain on my body is brutally punishing as well. With every tilt of the chair over the uneven path below, I have to counterbalance with my weight in the opposite direction. The equivalent of thousands of precisely timed abdominal contractions are taking their toll. This expanse of mud and the constant uphill climb are slowly eroding our confidence in our decision to make this five-hundred-mile pilgrimage. The final destination of Santiago de Compostela seems an eternity away. Yet, the Basque farmer's declaration—*the impossible is possible!*—resonates in our hearts as we continue to trudge through the thick, oozing mud.

| | |

— PATRICK —

Just when we think we've put the mud behind us, we are hit with another section of dark, wet muck. This next stretch seems even deeper than the first.

Slowly the wheels on Justin's chair keep turning as Ted strains against the red nylon harness with everything he has, trying desperately to keep the chair from sinking any deeper into the sludge.

My breath is now coming in ragged gasps as I push against the handlebars, with head down and arms outstretched, doing everything I can to keep us moving forward. I know that Justin is having a rough ride, but he resolutely calls out course corrections to us—"Go right! Now left!"—to help us avoid the worst obstacles and deep puddles along the way. Though we're all suffering, it's a true team effort, and it's drawing us together, even if we don't yet realize it.

Inch by inch, we work our way through this section and farther up the mountain, straining the wheels as the mud tries to swallow us from below. As we approach our third section of more than a hundred yards of mud, we see a small footpath where previous pilgrims have been able to easily bypass the mire. But it is too narrow for Justin's chair. We have no choice but to embrace the reality that sometimes the only way through something is *through* it.

Finally, we put the last section of mud behind us, but we're still on an upward slope with no end in sight. After climbing two hills in succession, we come to the high point of a third, and Ted shouts, "This is the top!"

But as Justin and I prepare for our first view of Spain, we see nothing but another hill stretching out before us. Onward we march, slowly and steadily climbing.

"Okay, this is it!" Ted exclaims at the top of the next rise. But there's still no summit to be found.

When one more "We're here!" turns out to be another premature celebration, Justin and I are still willing to give Ted a little bit of grace. But after the fourth and fifth false summits, we start yelling at him to shut up. This is more grueling than we'd imagined.

After ten and a half brutal hours, we are finally at the top of the Pyrenees Mountains, looking down into Spain.

Ted offers one last "Hey, guys, we're here!" but we're all too exhausted to laugh. It has already been a journey, and this is only the beginning. The joy of finally making it to the top and of being here with my best friend has me thinking about all the stories and adventures we'll get to tell our children.

When we retrieve Justin's phone to take a picture, we're surprised to see we have cell service. We call our wives.

"We made it to the top!" I say to Donna when she answers her phone.

"Thank God! We have been praying for you guys. The whole church is praying for you, but we thought you should have made it hours ago."

"So did we."

After we complete our calls, Justin asks, "If we have service, can we do a Facebook post from here?"

It turns out we can, and we laugh as I type the words for Justin, *Today I climbed a mountain in a wheelchair. What did you do?*

For a few more moments, we sit and enjoy the landscape. As I look around at the rolling hills, the green grass, and the trees in the valley below, it feels like the culmination of all the adventures Justin and I had as kids, many of which happened in the Deep Dirt Hills behind his house.

| | |

A mile and a half is a pretty short distance when you grow up in a small town where your parents let you ride your bike anywhere, at just about any time. I would often pedal my way to Justin's house to see what kind of fun we could muster up.

The Deep Dirt Hills were one of our childhood safe havens. It was a place to shoot BB guns, build forts, create adventures, and do some not-so-aggressive sledding in the winter—though at the time, we thought the hills we cascaded down were downright dangerous. We were putting our very lives at risk even attempting the steep descent.

Somehow, Justin and I found plenty of ways to get into trouble. It wasn't that we were *trying* to be delinquents. Our intentions were always pure . . . or at least grounded in curiosity.

I remember one winter day when we exhausted ourselves sledding and retreated to Justin's driveway with our friend Greg. The snow that day was perfect packing consistency, and before long a snowball-throwing contest was under way. First we aimed at Justin's mailbox across the street, but that was too easy, too close. So we took aim at his next-door neighbor's mailbox. Still too easy. So we upped the ante and set our sights on a new target: the basketball backboard in the Smiths' driveway, a little farther down the street.

The Smiths went to our church, and Mr. Smith taught with my dad at Ontario Junior High. He knew us well and wasn't terribly fond of our shenanigans—and for good reason.

My first attempt at the backboard wasn't even close. The nearly rock-hard snowball arced beautifully over the top of the backboard and crashed into the Smiths' garage door with a thundering *SLAM!*

Rather than do the sensible thing and run inside, we embraced our new target—the big white spot on Mr. Smith's brown garage door. Greg took a shot and was six feet too high, but the sound rang through the neighborhood. Justin went next and was three feet to the right. Five minutes later, the Smiths' garage door was polka-dotted with a dozen blotches of white. No one had won this contest, and everyone was about to lose.

As I firmed up my next snowball and prepared to heave it across the street, Mr. Smith came barreling out of the house, his face beet red, yelling at the top of his lungs: "What in the world do you think you're doing?"

"Having a snowball-throwing contest!" Greg replied.

Making a logical assumption that we were aiming at his backboard (this wasn't the first time), he pointed at it and shouted, "You guys aren't even close!"

Before I could stop myself, I shouted back the words that would seal our fate: "We weren't aiming for the backboard; we were aiming for your garage door!"

This is one of those moments that you wish you could take back. All three of us spent ample time grounded, and we were all relegated to our homes and rooms for remarkably similar lengths of time. I think our parents planned it that way.

On another occasion, my younger brother, Michael, and I were waiting for our parents after Wednesday night activities at church. Along with Justin, we had made a snow fort nestled in the bushes out near the road but invisible to anyone driving by. Naturally, a snowball-throwing contest ensued. The question was, who could hit a passing car closest to the church sign at the corner of the lot?

We'll never know the answer because we got only one throw—mine. It turns out ice balls and windshields don't get along. The sound of breaking glass and screeching brakes cut through the darkness. We ran so hard and so fast, straight into the church, up the stairs, out the fire escape, and into the safety of the field beyond.

I still feel bad about that one.

But not Mr. Smith's garage door.

That was just funny.

Time and time again, our curiosity and our willingness to be sucked into a dare got us into trouble. Justin once made a one-in-a-million shot with his BB gun when he sniped an unfortunate woman who was jogging by, all because his older brother had dared him to. I launched a bunch of crab apples from my slingshot into a backyard across the street and hit my neighbor in the face.

It seemed everything that went wrong could be traced back to a single question: *I wonder if I could . . . ?*

"I wonder if I could be the first one to hit that backboard?"

"I wonder if I could hit a moving car with a snowball?"

"I wonder if I can hit that lady with my BB gun?"

"I wonder how many crab apples I can shoot at one time from my slingshot?"

Here in the Pyrenees Mountains, standing by my best friend, I can hear those words as if I were there the day he uttered them.

"I wonder if I could do that in my wheelchair?"

"I wonder" questions brought us a lot of grief throughout our childhood years; but as adults, things have changed. Now, we balance wonder with calculated risk; we run the numbers and determine whether the *why* makes the *how* worth it.

As I stand alongside my best friend at the top of the Pyrenees Mountains, I realize that my *why* has evolved since Justin first told me about the Camino.

At first, it was simply because he asked me to go.

Then it was because people told us we'd never make it.

Though my *why* has changed, the *how* never has. It has always been *together*.

People often ask Justin and me what makes our friendship so strong. Our answer is simple: We choose to share life's adventures. I make his "I wonders" mine, and he makes my "I wonders" his. We pursue life together. We always have.

And now here we are, one long day and thirteen miles into a five-hundred-mile trek across northern Spain.

8

BLIND FAITH

— JUSTIN —

AN EARLY START TO our second day finds us on a nice, wide trail leading away from the town of Roncesvalles, Spain. It's raining again, and we all don our raincoats. We've already learned to appreciate the easier parts of the trail, and as we move along at a steady clip, the gravel crunches beneath my wheels in a cadence that is almost musical.

When we arrived in Roncesvalles last night, we were famished. Along with the four guys in the film crew, we descended upon a small restaurant, where we ordered four servings of lasagna, four large portions of ham and eggs, two orders of croquettes, two orders of french fries, and four large pizzas, washing it all down with cold beer. By the end of the meal, not a bite was left. As we headed to bed with full stomachs and sore muscles, we hoped for an easier day today.

This section of the Camino is increasingly wooded, but the canopy of trees isn't enough to shelter us from the rain. Periodically, Patrick or Ted will scout ahead to see what's coming around the next bend. Ted returns with news that a small river crosses the trail up ahead, and, of course, the bridge is too narrow. Filled with a hard-won confidence from all the obstacles we overcame yesterday, Patrick and Ted decide to push me across the river at a full run. Fortunately, the water is only about a foot deep.

Did I mention we're feeling confident?

Ted is now at the helm and Patrick is at my side, taking a breather from pushing.

"Guys, we just went over the Pyrenees with a wheelchair!" he says. "If we can do that, we've totally got this!"

No sooner has he uttered these words than our melodious cadence is rudely interrupted by a cascade of wrong notes. As Patrick starts to jog ahead to see what new obstacles the trail has in store for us, the sound of grinding metal erupts from beneath my chair, followed by what seems to be an explosion as the front wheel of my baby-jogger-on-steroids breaks off. The aluminum weld securing the wheel to the frame suffered so much abuse yesterday that it finally snapped. I am now sitting in a two-wheeled rickshaw several miles from the nearest town.

Running back toward us, Patrick yells, "You have got to be kidding me!" He bends down and picks up the broken wheel from the damp trail.

When Ted sees the jagged edge of the metal, he says, "Yeah, that's going to be a problem."

Repairing the wheel on the trail is not an option. We need a welder—and not just any welder. We need someone proficient at welding aluminum. As it begins to rain harder, Ted exclaims, "We have a man in a metal wheelchair, and a storm is coming. We have to get to shelter!"

As we discuss ways to keep the chair moving forward without the front stabilizing wheel, four sisters from Ireland start to pass us on the right. When Ted notices the vacant stare in one woman's eyes, he asks, "Are you blind?"

When the woman says yes, Ted replies, "Ah . . . well, great!"

What?

As I wince at Ted's response, he tries to dig himself out of the hole he's created.

"I mean, *congratulations*."

Not any better, Ted!

Fortunately, the women don't seem offended. As they continue on their way, Patrick says to Ted, "Did you just congratulate a woman for being blind?"

Eyes wide with embarrassment, Ted says emphatically, "No! I meant congratulations on doing the Camino."

Shaking his head and laughing, Patrick says, "Nice one, Ted!"

We begin moving forward with Patrick at the rear. While he continues to push my wheelchair, he now must also push down on the handlebars to keep the nose of the chair tilted upward, while Ted, at the front, pulls forward on my leg rest and simultaneously lifts it up to keep it from slamming into the back of his legs.

Another group of pilgrims approaches us—an elderly Spanish couple and their friend, who are walking short segments of the trail. Though I don't speak Spanish proficiently, I'm still able to understand most of what they say.

The wife, Emelia, tells us her husband has Parkinson's disease, which limits his ability to walk long distances, so instead they tackle a new section of the Camino every year. When they notice our predicament, they ask if there is some way they can help.

Between Ted and me, we use our broken Spanish and a Spanish/English dictionary to tell them we need to get to shelter.

They're not strong enough to help physically, but they walk alongside us to the next town as Patrick and Ted take turns pushing and pulling my two-wheeled contraption. It's a long two miles, but we make it with our new friends at our sides.

After inquiring with a local merchant, we head across the little town to a shop with a sign above the door that reads *Soldadura/ Panadería*.

Ted points to the sign and laughs.

"Does that say this is a welding shop *and* a bakery?"

"Uh, yes, it does," I reply.

Patrick walks to the door and pokes his head inside to verify. He comes back a minute later, chuckling to himself. "One half of the shop is welding equipment, and the other half has ovens and counter space."

We continue to laugh as we try to figure out the business model of this odd combination of services. When the young welder/baker comes out to look at the broken wheel, he quickly informs us that he doesn't weld aluminum. Aluminum welding is a very specific skill. The lower melting point and high heat conductivity of the metal make it tricky to get a good weld. The closest aluminum welder, he says, is in Pamplona, which is our destination for tomorrow.

Troubled by our plight, Emelia and her husband invite us to the home where they are staying, which is in the next town along the Camino route. We gratefully accept their invitation, and Patrick and Ted muscle my chair the distance, to a house where we are welcomed with hot coffee and cookies. Grateful to be out of the rain, we enjoy the next several hours of Spanish hospitality.

Now that we're dry and well cared for, we turn our attention to troubleshooting how to get to Pamplona. When we hear the exorbitant cost of a taxi, we decide to commandeer Robin's car—which is being used to transport the film gear from place to place. After the guys unload all the equipment and remove all but one of the backseats for my wheelchair to fit, Patrick lifts me into the passenger seat, arranges my legs, and buckles me in. After the chair is dismantled and loaded in the back of the car, Ted and Patrick have a very short discussion about who will drive.

"Without your glasses, you weren't able to tell the difference between mud and asphalt!" Ted exclaims.

"That was from a long distance!" Patrick replies.

I see Ted raise his eyebrows, as if to say, *Are we really having this conversation?*

"You need to be able to see things from a long distance to drive!"

"Good point," Patrick says as he crawls into the one remaining seat in the back. After we express our gratitude to our hosts and say good-bye to our new Spanish friends, Ted slides in behind the wheel, starts the engine, and we're off to Pamplona to find lodging and—with any luck—someone who can weld aluminum.

| | |

— PATRICK —

Although I'm wedged into the backseat, I'm able to help Ted navigate our way to Pamplona. It doesn't take long for us to cover the same distance by car that would have taken a day and a half to walk with Justin's wheelchair.

We had already planned to stay at a hotel in Pamplona, instead of in one of the albergues, and when they're able to adjust our reservation to accommodate our early arrival, we're happy we made that decision. Fortunately, the hotel has a spare hospital-type wheelchair we can use, and they offer us a place to lock up Justin's off-road chair while we look for a welder. Justin and I head up to our room while Ted drives back to pick up the film crew and gear.

Once the guys arrive, we put Robin and his fluent Spanish to work, calling anyone and everyone who welds in Pamplona. After two hours, we have no leads, so we give up the hunt and head out to buy some groceries.

Back in our room, we make some *bocadillos* (simple Spanish sandwiches consisting of meat and cheese on a baguette) and discuss our options for the next day. We have posted occasionally on Facebook since we've been in Europe, so our friends back home can follow our journey. As a result, the manufacturer of Justin's wheelchair has learned of our predicament and offered to send a replacement wheel. But this will take several days to arrive. Though it's great to have a backup plan, we need to be on the road sooner than five days from now.

As we brainstorm ways to find a welder, Justin says, "What about a bike shop? They have aluminum frames; maybe they know someone who can weld aluminum." We agree to pursue the possibility in the morning, but now it's time for bed. In spite of the stress and uncertainty, I find it surprisingly easy to fall asleep. Tomorrow will have answers; I just hope they're the ones we want.

| | |

The next morning, we head to a nearby café to grab some break-fast. When I return from purchasing our café con leches and two plates of ham and eggs, I see Justin looking at me over his shoulder.

"Did I do something wrong?" he asks.

"No, why?"

"So, why'd you put me in time-out then?" he says with a smile.

Sure enough, I'd been so focused on the task at hand that I didn't realize I had parked Justin off to the side in his chair, in a corner of the café where his only view was the wall. Shaking my head sheepishly, all I can do is apologize.

"I'm so sorry. I guess I was a little absentminded. What can I say? I was hungry."

After breakfast, Ted and I take turns, one of us pushing Justin in the borrowed wheelchair toward downtown Pamplona, while the other pushes the broken one alongside. Just as we locate the bike shop, the staff walks out for siesta. In Spain, this could last anywhere from thirty minutes to three hours—if they come back at all. So, instead, we walk into a medical supply shop next door, where—as luck would have it—we meet Ramón, who knows a few things about welding and who happens to be visiting his girlfriend, who works there. Ramón examines the broken wheel before telling us that he doesn't weld aluminum—but he offers to call a friend who does.

Ten minutes later, Ramón's friend is turning the wheel over in his hands and declaring it *"demasiado complicado"*—too complicated. Ramón makes another phone call to another friend, but still no luck. The calls continue, and we find ourselves in a game of "six degrees of the aluminum welder in Pamplona." After too many calls to count, Ramón finds someone who might be able to help us.

Justin, Ted, and I head out the door to tell the film crew the plan, and as we walk outside, I make the mistake of commenting to Jasper about a pretty woman across the street.

"Are you serious?" he asks.

"Yeah, she's pretty."

Jasper howls with laughter and says, "Dude! That's a man in a dress!"

I really wish I had my glasses.

Armed with a plan, we are excited to get back to the Camino. But our trip to the welder will have to wait. Robin parked illegally back at the hotel, and his car has been towed, so we wait while he and Terry go to pay the €200 fine and retrieve the vehicle.

Could this day get any worse?

After we've waited for an hour, Robin arrives and we load the wheelchair into the back of his car. Robin, Mike, and I set out for the welder's shop, while Justin and Ted head back to the hotel to get some rest.

Riding with Robin at the wheel is an adventure. In spite of the fact that I have a map in my lap and the destination circled in red, Robin pulls over every mile or so and asks for directions from anyone he can find. He shouts for the attention of people walking by on the sidewalk, people on bicycles, and even fellow drivers. At one point, he flags down a gentleman driving in the opposite direction. As the cars slowly roll past each other in the middle of a busy street, Robin is too engrossed in conversation to notice the pedestrian he hits. Fortunately, this happens at the breakneck speed of four miles per hour, and no harm is done.

We finally arrive at the shop, unload the wheelchair, and take it inside to the fabricator who we hope will solve our problem. As he runs his finger slowly along the broken weld, I can see he is deep in thought. Nervous about leaving $8,000 worth of aluminum in the hands of a complete stranger, I turn to Robin and say, "Ask him if he can fix it."

Robin poses the question, and the gentleman responds in rapid-fire Spanish.

"He says, 'Come back at ten o'clock tomorrow and find out.'"

| | |

The next morning, with ten o'clock rapidly approaching, I climb into the passenger seat of Robin's car while Jasper slides into the seat behind me. We make our way toward the fabrication shop, but none of the buildings look familiar.

"Are you sure we're going the right way?" I ask Robin.

He assures me we're on the right track, but after thirty minutes of driving, Robin resigns himself to the fact that we are completely lost. Employing his method of getting directions, he flags down a man on the sidewalk and asks for help. Turns out we've driven to the opposite corner of Pamplona. Robin gets his directions and hurriedly flips a U-turn, cutting off a car behind us—which, as you might expect when things are going wrong, belongs to two traffic officers.

The lights flash on, the siren sounds, and we are pulled over. It doesn't take long to realize we are in the middle of a classic good cop/bad cop scenario.

Good Cop approaches the driver's window and begins talking to Robin in rapid Spanish. Robin replies apologetically and engages the officer in conversation.

"What's going on?" I ask. "What are you saying to him?"

"I'm explaining what we're doing in Spain, and I told him why we need to get to the fabrication shop."

As Robin continues to talk with Good Cop, he stops periodically to catch me up on the conversation. At one point, he mentions the documentary and points to Jasper, who is filming the encounter from the backseat.

When Bad Cop sees this, he comes unglued and begins yelling at Jasper.

Jasper, who speaks fluent French but only a little Spanish, turns to Robin for help.

"It's illegal to film the police in Spain," Robin says, "so you need to turn off the camera . . . and you need to get out of the car."

I'm usually pretty levelheaded, but right now my head is spinning.

While Jasper gets out of the car and Bad Cop runs his passport, Good Cop is still in conversation with Robin, who seems remarkably calm for having just been told the consequences for filming a police officer—a €5,000 fine and potential jail time. I don't know if this is true or whether Good Cop is just trying to scare us, but Robin turns on some magical charm and continues talking about the broken wheelchair and our need to get to the fabrication shop.

As Bad Cop reads Jasper the riot act, something comes over Good Cop, and he yells something in Spanish to his partner. The conversation suddenly turns. I don't know what has happened, but I choose to believe it is a little divine intervention, because now Bad Cop is asking us where we're headed and is offering to escort us.

Totally bewildered, Jasper gets back in the car, and we follow the officers through the streets of Pamplona. Thirty minutes later, we arrive at the fabrication shop, and the welder proudly presents us with a repaired wheelchair. As I examine the new weld, I look up at the man responsible for the repair.

"¡Muchas gracias, señor!"

9

MEASURE TWICE, CUT ONCE

— JUSTIN —

PATRICK'S EXCURSION WITH Pamplona's finest has cost us a fair amount of time. As a result, our departure is much later than we'd hoped. We're grateful to be back on the trail, but we know we're looking at a late arrival in Uterga, tonight's destination, about eleven and a half miles to the west.

The sun's warmth radiates against our backs as we walk through the city of Pamplona, a surprisingly accessible metropolis of about 200,000 people. We easily navigate the many streets, sidewalks, and parks as we follow the little yellow arrows that mark the Camino path. Before long, we arrive at the trailhead on the southwest side of town, and we're glad to be back on the dirt path. But there is a bit of fear and trepidation about the new weld. It looks sturdy enough, but the real proof is in its performance, and we have a long way to go.

As we work our way farther from town, the trail meanders through a series of rolling hills, but up ahead we see a sizable climb in our immediate future. As we struggle up a section with an abundance of loose rocks underfoot, a cyclist blurs past us, shouting, *"¡Buen Camino!"* This standard greeting for every pil-grim on the trail—"Good walk!"—creates a unique and instant bond among fellow travelers.

When the Italian cyclist reaches the top of the grade, he stops, lays down his bike at the side of the trail, and jogs back down the hill to give us a hand.

Stepping in as copilot next to Patrick in the back, he helps push while Ted pulls on the harness out front. It's a short but strenuous climb, and all three human engines grunt and groan as they propel me up the hill.

At the top of the incline, I use my basic Italian to thank the cyclist and wish him good travels, but before he leaves us, we reach a fork in the trail, which initiates an entirely new conver-sation about the best way to go. After a brief discussion, punctu-ated by copious hand gestures, we decide to stay on the footpath rather than taking the bike route. We wave good-bye to our new friend as he heads off to the right while we proceed left.

Continuing up the now gentle grade, we are soon greeted by an impressive sea of green and red—beautiful poppies covering the hillsides as far as we can see. As we draw closer, we realize our path cuts directly across one of these poppy fields. Instead of a trail wide enough for my wheelchair, we face a narrow foot-path, running east to west. Embracing what lies before us, we forge ahead.

Progress is slow, and we begin to wonder whether this is even part of the trail. The ground is incredibly uneven, and the path is littered with rocks the size of cantaloupes. My chair is twenty-four inches wide, and the path is maybe half that. This means that most of the time, both of the mountain bike tires are rolling against the resistance of three-foot-tall poppies. Additionally, the trail is so uneven that Patrick must constantly lift up one side of the handlebars to keep me from tipping over, while Ted pulls on my footrest and lifts the front wheel over ruts, rocks, and holes to protect our new weld. Every so often, the two switch places to give their fatigued muscles a break.

We begin to wonder whether we should turn back and look for an alternate route, but we are now halfway through the field, and turning my chair around amid the thick growth of poppies will be nearly impossible. So we continue to fight our way through. Finally, we reach the other side and are back on a clearly marked trail, where the familiar yellow arrows point the way toward Santiago. We've read that if we go for too long without seeing one of these arrows, we're probably lost, so we're happy to see a large stone pillar directly in front of us with a yellow arrow pointing to the left.

The path is now wider, and we are excited at the prospect of reaching Alto de Perdón, a monument to all the pilgrims who have walked the Camino for over a thousand years. In our guidebook, we've seen pictures of the oxidized-metal silhouettes depicting pilgrims on foot, on horseback, and leading pack animals, arrayed in a caravan across the top of a plateau, and we're eager to see it with our own eyes. Soon we catch a glimpse of it in the distance, and we begin the ascent.

Thirty feet from the top, we hit loose rock, and Patrick has to get down on all fours to gain enough leverage to pull while Ted continues to push me toward the apex of the hill. When we reach the top, we realize the monument is even more impressive than it appears in pictures—a work of art on display in a windy, open-air museum, stretching more than one hundred feet across the hilltop.

After the arduous climb, we're happy to find a fountain with fresh, cool drinking water. While I enjoy a few minutes of respite looking down over Pamplona in the distance, Patrick and Ted drain and refill our water bottles and the water reservoir in my backpack.

The monument seems to stare back at me, and I think to myself, *They need to add a silhouette of a guy in a wheelchair.*

My musing is interrupted by thoughts of our next challenge. A few pilgrims we've met along the way have warned us about the section of trail leading toward Uterga. The steep downhill grade and large, loose rocks create dangerous terrain for a wheelchair. Consulting the map in our guidebook for an alternate route, we see a country road leading down the hill to our right, past a ridge-line studded with evenly spaced wind turbines. Taking the road all the way into town will add a fair amount of time, so we decide to go as far as the bottom of the hill and then cut across on a short trail identified on the map. Anticipating this next stretch will be rather uneventful, the film crew goes on ahead to find a place to stay the night.

With Patrick now pulling back on the handlebars to slow our descent, and Ted as an anchor behind him, I'm reminded of our last day of training on Quail Ridge. The steep road soon has us moving at a fairly quick pace, despite Ted and Patrick's short, calculated steps. Off to our right, the massive windmills spin slowly, and the rhythmic sound of their blades slicing through the air marks the tempo for Patrick and Ted as they march down the hill. We make it to the short trail and take the cutoff, ignoring the absence of yellow arrows.

"Are we sure this is right?" Ted asks.

"No, but it definitely heads in the right direction," Patrick replies. "Should we stay on the road?"

Not sure what to do, but wanting to avoid the extra distance the road will add to our already long day, we set a course we hope will get us back to the trail at a point below the loose rock slope.

"Let's see where this goes," I say to Ted and Patrick.

For a good mile—and an hour's worth of work—the trail is wide and the up and down of the hills is minimal, but the terrain is reminiscent of the rough trail we fought through the Pyrenees, and the tall trees on either side make it difficult to keep our bearings. Judging by the wide tire ruts all along the way, we determine early on that this must be a popular jeep or off-road vehicle trail.

The lack of yellow arrows should have concerned us, but when we started down this path, we were fairly certain it headed straight to the base of the steep downhill section we wanted to avoid. We're less certain now.

The second mile on this "shortcut" begins to drift to the left, and with each successive hill we're actually gaining elevation. Our conversation dies away as the prospect of a shortcut has turned into anything but.

The brush and grass have gradually thickened, and I now have bunches of dried vegetation stuck in the spokes of my tires and wrapped around the axles. Patrick clenches his jaw as he mulls over the situation while pulling out the debris.

Both he and Ted have been taking turns running ahead to make sure we can continue. When Ted is out ahead on one of these sorties, he yells back, "The grass and growth are getting even thicker and taller the farther I go. I don't think anyone has been through here in a long time."

"Can we make it through in the chair?" Patrick yells back.

"I think so! We have to be close!"

When Ted returns, both he and Patrick are covered in sweat. Patrick asks me if I want to turn back.

"We've made it this far, let's see where this goes," I reply.

Ted jumps in behind my chair to give Patrick a break from pushing, and Patrick attempts to clear a path for my wheels by stomping down the growth that pushes back against my tires. With the higher elevation, we can now see the western horizon to our right, and we're certain we're heading in the right direction. But it's anyone's guess where we'll come out on the trail.

As the trees begin to thin, we reach a wide spot connecting to the steep downhill portion of the Camino. Looking up to our left, we discover that our two-hour "shortcut" has saved us only the first thirty feet of the downhill stretch we were desperately trying to avoid in the first place.

Ted's shoulders sag, and Patrick hangs his head in defeat. I just lean back in my wheelchair and take a deep breath.

"Well, we found the trail!" Ted says as he turns to look at Patrick and me.

"At least we know we're not lost!" I hear from behind me. Ted begins to laugh, and it isn't long before Patrick and I join him.

| | |

— PATRICK —

I remember my grandfather as a remarkable woodworker. Like Justin with his artwork, my grandfather's patience and attention to detail have always impressed me, even as a young boy. For the most part, my exposure to his work was the finished product. A beautiful china hutch sat in our dining room, and a grandfather clock stood in our living room. Every time the clock chimed, I was reminded of the hard work that Grandpa had put in to create such a gorgeous piece of furniture.

When we were old enough, my parents let each of us kids spend a week of the summer with our grandparents in nearby Meridian. A week apart from Justin meant he and I had to delay any plans for mischief, but my grandparents' country homestead, complete with a six-thousand-square-foot house, large red barn, and massive garden, was an acceptable tradeoff. I did, however, have to work while I was there. I spent days pulling weeds in the garden, picking ripe berries, or doing whatever other chores they came up with. In addition to a good work ethic, my grandpa taught me a valuable life lesson that I would never forget but would sometimes ignore, to my own detriment.

One particular summer day when I was about nine, the day's work was completed and my grandfather asked me to accompany him down to his shop in the basement of their home. He had already taught me how to play chess, and now he wanted to teach me a thing or two about woodworking. The subterranean room he had dedicated to his craft was incredible—about a thousand square feet filled with every tool you could imagine. Most of them looked ancient to me, but all were in perfect working order. His table saw, dating back to the 1950s, still ran like a champ.

Guiding me over to a workbench, he showed me an array of boards and nails, and laid out simple, clear instructions for building a bird feeder, which was the task at hand.

"No matter what, measure twice and cut once!" he said. "This applies to woodworking and people!" he added with a smile. With that admonition firmly in mind, we began our collective work. I measured and cut while my grandfather made sure I didn't remove any fingers during the process.

Details have never been my strong point, especially as a child. Working hard while overlooking the details has often led me down the wrong path. As I cut a piece of wood for the base of my bird feeder, my grandpa watched with little expression on his face. With all the pieces cut, I began to assemble my woodworking masterpiece, only to discover the base was about an inch too narrow.

"You measured once!" Grandpa said with a hint of a smile. "And now you have to cut twice!"

"I measured twice!" I argued.

"No, you didn't. I watched you."

He knew I had made the mistake, but he let me continue down the path until I discovered it on my own. He could have intervened, but chose not to. Rather than simply cutting a new piece, my grandpa made me start over from the beginning, measuring and cutting each piece again. This was one of the few times I was ever angry with him. He let me fail and then almost laughed about it. But now, as an adult, I know he wasn't laughing. He was silently celebrating how this lesson would one day serve me well.

I wish I had heeded his advice on the Camino.

| | |

As we begin our descent, we're all three saying things like "Shortcuts never pay off!" and "Measure twice, cut once!" It turns out we misread the map and took the wrong road. On top of that, we ignored the clear warning the absence of yellow arrows should have provided. The sun is just beginning to touch the horizon, and we still have a long way to go.

Ted is now at the helm behind Justin, pulling against the gravity of the chair, while I am strapped in behind Ted, leaning back into the nylon harness that runs across my back and is attached to the back of the chair with two carabiners. Painstakingly, we work our way down the hill, zigzagging from left to right and back again to avoid the large rocks and to keep too much momentum from building. When we finally reach the bottom, Ted takes a break and I push Justin down the flat, wide trail toward Uterga.

"No more shortcuts!" Justin shouts into the gathering twilight. Ted and I just laugh.

At dusk, we reach our destination, only to find all the inns are full. Terry was able to secure lodging for himself, but albergues don't hold beds for pilgrims. It's a first-come, first-served business model, and we are dead last. Frustrated, but resigned to the necessity of moving on, we retrieve our headlamps from our backpacks and begin the three-mile trek to the town where Mike, Jasper, and Robin are spending the night.

With the wind picking up, the temperature begins to drop, so we stop briefly to bundle Justin against the cold. Heading straight into the wind, I suddenly realize how incredibly tired I am. Surrendering the handlebars to Ted to push Justin onward to the town of Obanos, I drop back and moderate my pace, grateful to be able to just walk for a while. In the darkening countryside, I'm thinking of my grandpa and the bird feeder. As a smile crosses my face, lightning illuminates the sky to our left, marking the approach of another storm. My thoughts scatter with a renewed sense of urgency, and we push on.

By the time we reach Obanos, the darkness of the night makes the town roads difficult to navigate. Even though Terry called ahead to let the other guys know we're coming, we have no idea where to find them. Around ten thirty, with our lamps on high beam and a stroke of luck, we stumble across our film crew in the heart of town. Tired, grumpy, and hungry, we find some food. After the usual routine of getting Justin into our room, we settle in for the rest and recuperation we so desperately need.

As I drift off to sleep, my mind wanders through the events of the day—the challenges, the shortcut, back to thoughts of my grandfather—and finally rests on God.

Many people grab on to a concept of God as judgmental and angry, as someone who causes strife simply to teach us lessons or toy with us. I don't profess to understand the creator of the universe, but I have no time for a divine puppeteer who throws obstacles in our way for his own amusement. The God I believe in is a God of love and compassion, much like a loving parent or my wise grandfather.

My grandpa didn't set me up for failure, but he didn't intervene to keep me from making a mistake. He simply used my birdfeeder mishap to teach me an incredibly valuable lesson—take time, evaluate, and learn from my mistakes.

Today was a frustrating day, and the challenges could easily have been avoided. But even though I ignored the lesson I had learned from my grandfather, being reminded of the wisdom that can dwell in simple tasks affirms so much of what we've done.

I don't know exactly what my grandpa meant when he said, "No matter what, measure twice and cut once! This applies to woodworking and people!" but I'm pretty sure today qualifies. We didn't measure twice by double-checking the map, and we ignored the absence of yellow arrows. As a result, our shortcut was anything but short. Yet so often in life, it's easy to take the path of least resistance in hopes of something easier around the next bend.

I don't believe that God litters our lives with obstacles, but he certainly doesn't just take them away or prevent us from making wrong decisions. He lets us walk the path we choose, and he lets us encounter the struggles of life, hoping we will learn and grow from each experience.

Today I'm grateful for this.

No more shortcuts!

10

PADDY WAGON AND SKEEZ

— PATRICK —

JUSTIN AND I HAVE BEEN together twenty-four hours a day for the past ten days, and we've also had Ted and the film crew by our sides. Despite the challenges of the Pyrenees, the broken wheel, getting lost, and our constant and intense proximity, our spirits are high.

Since our run-in with the Spanish police, we have taken to calling Robin "The Fixer." He solves problems, gets us out of tight situations, and makes sure the cameras and equipment are running smoothly. We didn't come up with that nickname on a whim; he earned it, and it's a name he clearly enjoys.

Robin isn't the only one with a nickname on the Camino. Ted is a beast—not because of his size but because of his fierce determination, strength, and willpower—and we've all begun referring to him as "Team Ted." He may be only one individual, but he gets as much done as a team of people.

Team Ted recently began calling me Paddy after hearing it from Justin over the past week. And Justin has been Skeez for as long as I can remember.

Paddy and Skeez—there's something powerful in nicknames that become terms of endearment. There's a history behind any nickname that sticks for as long as ours have. And we're reminded of their origin every time we hear them.

| | |

— JUSTIN —

My father, Jim, is the original Skeez, dating back to his college days, but Patrick felt it worked for me as well while we were growing up, and the name stuck. It wasn't long before all our friends knew me as Skeez.

Patrick, on the other hand, had no familial history of nicknames. So I worked with what I had—and thus began a litany of iterations of Patrick's name. Some lasted only a moment; others a few weeks or months. I believe the order went something like this:

"Patricia?"

Nope. Apparently that falls into the realm of insult.

"Patty Melt?"

Nope.

"Patio Furniture?"

Nope.

"Paddy McGroin?"

A tip of the cap to Patrick's Irish ancestry. But nope.

"Paddy McCrotch?"

Nope, for all the same reasons.

"Spatty?"

This worked for a while, but just didn't seem to fit the way I wanted it to.

"Paddy Wagon?"

We found a winner! I don't know why it stuck, but it did, and I started calling him Paddy Wagon everywhere we went. Patrick didn't seem to mind, and the name never really got old. Paddy Wagon and Skeez—that's how we were known for years. But just because something works doesn't mean there isn't a better option out there somewhere.

I don't recall exactly when it happened, but it was sometime during our middle school years. One of us had just returned from a summer family vacation, so we had been apart longer than our usual twenty-four-hour limit. If I remember correctly, Patrick had just arrived in my driveway on his bicycle, and I was pretty excited to see him. I don't know what came over me, but I squinted my eyes and tilted my head back while out of my mouth erupted a loud, high-pitched, and prolonged "PAA-DDY!"

As Patrick walked toward me, his head dropped slightly forward and began to turn from side to side. I could see the rise and fall of his shoulders as he laughed. There it was—the pitch-perfect name that had eluded me for so long. I had been so close and had finally found the name that would stick forever.

Out here on the Camino, he hears Paddy more often than Patrick, and he wouldn't have it any other way.

| | |

The past few days have been especially rough on my backside, lower back, and neck. In an effort to give my body and wheelchair a break from the rugged trail, we decide to travel along a paved road that parallels the path of the Camino. Shortly after leaving Obanos, we work our way from the trail onto pavement.

As soon as we get out on the road, a cyclist speeds past us, shouting, *"¡Buen Camino!"* But he's moving much faster than any other cyclist we've met.

Within seconds, four more cyclists power past us, and it doesn't take long to realize we're in the middle of a bike race—and clearly not competing. Over the next few minutes, sixty or more cyclists rush past us in their pursuit of those up ahead; and for the next two hours, as the sun beats down on our backs and radiates off the pavement, this same stream of cyclists keeps passing by. Apparently they're riding some kind of loop. Each time they pass, the cheers and shouts of *"¡Buen Camino!"* get louder and grow in number. The joy in their voices distracts us from the heat and our sore feet.

A scattering of their fans along the roadside also cheer us on, and now we're laughing at the situation because we've tried multiple times to find a way back to the Camino path, to no avail. Instead, we continue to press forward, in the middle of the race, staying to the left side of the road while cyclists whiz by on our right.

As Ted and Patrick begin powering my chair up a long hill, we see two tables with sunshades at the top. After a slow and steady climb, we approach the summit and can see that one of the tables is covered in bananas, cut in half, and the other is stocked with shiny packets of energy gel reflecting in the sun. Several volunteers stand at the ready, passing out bananas for cramps and gel packs for energy to the fatigued cyclists.

As we begin to crest the hill, the volunteers cheer and clap for us while filling our pockets with banana halves and packets of the not-so-tasty energy gel. Ted and Patrick are repeatedly smacked on the back and shoulders by strangers who are smiling and shouting out words of encouragement in Spanish. Many of these same people hug me in my chair and give me looks of admiration. We are laughing at how crazy this day is, and we're overjoyed by the reception we receive from these complete strangers.

Now on a flat stretch of road, we finally leave the bike race behind, making our way back onto a smooth section of the Camino trail, and continue our day's journey to Estella. When we arrive in town, we find lodging and get cleaned up before dinner. Ted and Patrick have angry feet from the hard pavement, so they exchange their sweaty shoes for the flip-flops they have stuffed in their backpacks.

Estella is a beautiful town, and the central plaza buzzes with the happy sounds of local denizens who are out for dinner and drinks after a long day's work. As we sit at an outdoor table enjoying a cold beer, other pilgrims filter into town, and a couple of Germans we met briefly on the trail from Pamplona join us at our table.

Ziggy and Dietmar, both in their sixties, are brothers walking a section of the Camino. Dietmar is taking his brother on the pilgrimage for his birthday. Their trek is ending soon, and this is one of the last times we'll see them. We welcome the opportunity to enjoy dinner with these new friends before they return home. As we eat, we recount for them the details of our inadvertent entry in the bike race, and we all have a good laugh at our incredible circumstances.

| | |

— PATRICK —

With the sun hanging low in the sky and shadows beginning to swallow up the town square, I excuse myself to take a bathroom break. When I return, everyone at the table is deeply engrossed in animated conversation. Justin looks up, and as we make eye contact, he smiles and shouts out, "PAA-DDY!" in that unique, high-pitched way of his—like two half notes on the upper register of the piano, descending from D-sharp to C-sharp.

I can't help but tilt my head down, shake it from side to side, and laugh. Justin laughs with me, and the joy on his face is infectious. By the time I reach the table, he is leaning forward in his chair and laughing so hard that his eyes have smiles all their own.

Paddy and Skeez may just be silly names from our childhood—but every time Justin calls me Paddy, I am taken back to riding bikes across town, snowball mishaps, shared groundings for shared mischief, and any of a number of moments we have crafted together.

Right now, though, I'm taken back just a few hours to finding ourselves in the middle of a bike race on the Camino de Santiago.

Who we are has grown by one more memory. We have grown by one more story, one more shared experience, one more adventure.

11

TAKING THE BULL BY THE HORNS

— JUSTIN —

TODAY'S STOP, LOS ARCOS, is a small town between Estella and Logroño, about forty miles west of Pamplona. It has taken us six days to make it this far, but this section of the Camino is relatively uneventful and goes by quickly.

With an intense sun beating down on our heads and shoulders, we enter the town square—Plaza de Santa María—and are greeted with applause from many of the pilgrims we have met along the way as they sit at tables in the center of the square, enjoying cold beer and food from the nearby cafés. With the sun still high overhead, Patrick orders food for the three of us, and we sit outside the Church of Santa María, enjoying a light afternoon breeze.

While we eat, we learn from our fellow pilgrims that the town's 1,100 or so residents are about to spend the evening running with bulls. In just a few short hours, this courtyard will be fenced off and large bulls will be turned loose to lumber through the streets and throughout the square, while smaller, more aggressive bulls chase down whoever stands in their path.

This we have to see!

We were in Pamplona much too early to witness the Festival of San Fermín, known for its running of the bulls. But now, as luck would have it, we're about to have front-row seats for a different version of running with bulls. Uncertain about how the festivities will be organized, we decide to wait right where we are in the square.

"Can you take our packs and check us in at one of the albergues?" Patrick asks Ted. "We'll stay here and save us a spot to watch this."

"Sure!" Ted responds. "I can't believe we're going to get to watch a bunch of idiots get chased by bulls!"

As afternoon approaches evening, the number of people in the plaza seems to double every fifteen minutes or so. Soon a group of men begin moving seven-foot-tall sections of thick fencing into place at the end of the square, blocking the archway that leads to where Ted has gone to look for lodging. Side streets are soon barricaded, and a Spanish gentleman approaches us to let us know we're not safe where we're seated. Seeking his advice about a better location, we are directed to a section along the north side of the square, opposite the church, where a number of people have already gathered. Patrick steps in behind my chair, releases the brakes, and we relocate to the designated safe area.

The crowd continues to grow, and soon the same men who barricaded the streets are lining our spectators' section with similar fencing. We haven't thought this through. It is now four thirty in the afternoon, we're completely fenced in, and the fence will not come down till after seven.

"Looks like we're watching the whole thing," I say to Patrick.

After successfully securing beds for all three of us, Ted returns just as the festivities are about to begin. At five o'clock, a bell sounds and two massive brown-and-white bulls come trotting down a side street to our left. Cheers explode from the crowd around us. The men in the square begin to wave their hands, hats, and shirts to get the attention of these huge animals, but the beasts show little interest. Then another bell rings, and the real excitement begins. Two more bulls appear—smaller, but moving much faster. These two are much more inclined to be enticed by the many attempts to get their attention.

Soon, the thirty or so men out in the square are voluntarily placing themselves in the path of danger, and we begin to understand what kind of game is afoot. The idea is to touch the horn of a bull without getting knocked down or gored. Near miss after near miss, the bulls charge and people dance out of the way. Finally, we hear the crowd explode as a young man successfully grabs a horn while dodging another bull's charge. Seeing this, I turn to Patrick and say, "You should go out there! When will you ever have another chance to run with bulls?"

"Are you kidding?" he says. "Those things are huge. And if I get gored, you're screwed!"

"Don't worry," I say with a smile, "I have Ted."

Ted looks at me kind of funny. "I'm only here for a few more days," he says, "and if Paddy gets hurt, you really are screwed!"

I continue to work on them, and before long they are second-guessing their decision to take the safe route.

Looking out at the square, Patrick says, "It's true we'll never have this chance again. You only live once, right?"

Turning to Ted, he says, "But we can't both get hurt. Only one of us can go."

"Then it should be you," Ted says with a smile.

As Patrick begins to climb the fence to enter the plaza, I'm laughing to myself. He has always been one for an adrenaline rush. Whether rock climbing or jumping off cliffs, he has always had a little thrill-seeking in his blood. But honestly, I didn't think he would take the bait.

| | |

— PATRICK —

When Justin and I entered ninth grade, I went out for the football team. Our high school didn't yet have a soccer program, so Justin waited for spring to play tennis.

At six feet three inches, I was tall for a freshman, but I weighed only 145 pounds—not exactly the classic frame for a football player. Still, I enjoyed the game, and even though I wasn't very fast, I had decent hands. That first year, I saw some playing time as wide receiver, but with daily practices and weekly games, I had a lot less time to spend with Justin during the season.

Before the start of our sophomore year, I hatched a plan to get more time with my best friend. Since Justin wasn't involved in a fall sport, I told him it only made sense for him to join me on the football field.

"Think how much time we'll have together!" I said. "And we'll be in excellent shape for the ladies."

Though Justin initially rejected my brilliant suggestion, I eventually wore him down after weeks of badgering. He decided to join the team just in time for two-a-day practices, which commenced a couple of weeks before the start of school. The combination of summer heat and intense physical activity had us both shedding pounds from our already lean frames and eating food by the plateful.

Despite Justin's small size and lack of football experience, the coaches put him on the defensive line, while at six foot three and 155 pounds, I continued playing wide receiver. Though it's difficult to admit, I wasn't very good, but somehow I made the team two years in a row. Justin, however, was terrible. In hindsight, I feel kind of bad for talking him into playing, but at the time I was just glad there was someone worse than me on the field.

Every practice seemed to start or end with all the players gathered in a multilayered circle, with the coaches in the middle. This massive huddle, with the biggest and meanest players always closest to the center, was a source of deep-seated fear for both Justin and me. Inevitably, the coaches would vacate the middle of the circle and initiate a drill known as "bull in the ring."

When the coach called out a player's name, that player would enter the center of the circle, and when the whistle blew, his job was to lower his shoulders and hit any player who challenged him—which always seemed to be one of the biggest guys. As two of the scrawniest players on the team, Justin and I were both petrified at the possibility of hearing our names and having to step into the ring. Somehow, Justin escaped this fate, but I wasn't so lucky. On more than one occasion, I suffered a beatdown from players who seemed twice my size.

To this day, I wonder whether Justin still harbors some mild resentment toward me for convincing him to play football. On the other hand, allowing your best friend to talk you into a situation where you find yourself entirely outmatched makes for great stories and even better life lessons. I take this hope with me as I scale the fence.

| | |

As I drop to the stone-paved surface of the plaza, a small voice screams in my head: *What in the world are you doing?* But Justin's persuasive words are considerably louder, and I'm actually thinking, *I've got this!*

For the past hour, I've been studying the various techniques of the men in the plaza who have successfully dodged the advancing bulls. As near as I can tell, there are two recipes for success. One is to convince one of these large animals to chase you and then dive out of the way at the last possible moment. The second strategy is to stand in the path of a charging bull, fake a step to one side as the bull approaches to get him to slightly change direction, and then lunge in the opposite direction as the bull goes by.

As I stand at the west end of the plaza, with the church to my right and safety on the other side of the fence to my left, a surge of adrenaline begins to work its way through my bloodstream. I can feel the slight tingling sensation and jitteriness grow. When two shadows appear on either side of me, I realize I am no longer alone. Glancing to my right, I see Ted.

"What are you doing out here?" I shout.

He just smiles and says, "Justin told me to do it."

I can't argue with that.

To my left, I find Mike, with a camera.

"I'm catching this on film!" he says.

It's too late to challenge their decision to join me. The moment I look toward the other end of the plaza, I see the two larger bulls running off to the left around a corner while the two smaller, more aggressive bulls come charging in our direction. A bare-chested man waving his shirt distracts one of the bulls, but the other is lumbering straight toward us. In an instant, Mike bolts for the fence with Ted right on his heels, and I'm left standing there—alone again. For the briefest moment, I can see Justin looking at me through a gap in the fence, but I can't tell if he's terrified for me or laughing his brains out.

With the beast now ten feet away, I lunge to my right—just like I practiced it in my mind—to convince the bull to change direction. He shifts slightly but still has me dead center between his twelve-inch horns. As I jump back to my left, I see him lower his head, ready for the gore.

Panicked now, I begin an incredibly uncoordinated pirouette—but as my head and body rotate to the left, my feet are slow to follow.

"Ohhhhh nooooo!" I shout as I lower my right hand to chest level in an effort to push myself away from the half-ton of mayhem that is about to collide with my body.

For a fraction of a second, my hand lands on the bull's horn as its massive shoulder brushes my rib cage.

He missed!

With limbs moving in all directions, I flail my way back to the fence and scramble up and over like a deranged spider monkey. When my feet touch ground on the safe side of the fence, I hear nothing but laughter. Ted is laughing. Mike is laughing. Robin is laughing. Complete strangers are laughing and smacking me on the back. But no one is laughing as loud or as hard as Justin.

"Dude, your eyes were the size of silver dollars!" he shouts. "I can't believe he didn't get you. That was awesome!" Justin hunches over in his chair as laughter consumes him.

Robin steps to my side and says in his thick French accent, "You touched a horn!"

"Does it count if I didn't mean to?"

Pointing across the square at a couple of young men, he tells me to listen. I can't make out everything they're saying, but I do hear the words *americano* and *estúpido*.

"Are they calling me stupid?" I ask Robin.

He shakes his head and says, "Not exactly. They're calling you a 'stupid macho American.' Another pilgrim tried the same thing last night and was taken to the hospital because he was gored. You were lucky."

I don't know what to make of what just happened. Justin just talked me into doing one of the dumbest things of my life, and I put up little resistance. I can't help but wonder whether, on some level, this is payback for football. I guess we're even.

— JUSTIN —

I will never forget the look on Patrick's face when he realized Ted was standing next to him out there among the bulls, or the size of his eyes when he began to move in a way that seemed to defy the laws of physics. I didn't know a person's toes could point in one direction while his head and torso were going the opposite way. But I'm glad he didn't get hurt, and I'm glad he seized the opportunity.

Patrick knows this, but I would have given anything to have been out there in the fray with him. I love my life and am grateful for everything I get to experience. But in times like these, I can't deny there's a sting. I want to be out there running with the bulls, risking my life alongside Patrick for a good story. But in these moments, I have a choice: I can let my limits ruin me, or I can let them go. If I can't catch a bull by its horn, the next best thing is to watch my best friend do it for me.

Patrick and I have often found ourselves outmatched by our circumstances. But we've learned that if we live in fear and never try, if we never attempt something scary or daunting, we can't know what limits we possess. If we don't push ourselves, the only limits we face are the ones we place on ourselves, the ones we fabricate in our minds.

It may sound simplistic, or even ridiculous, but something was triggered in Patrick today. His near miss with the bull was validation that he is capable of far more than he thinks he is. He doesn't know it yet, but change is coming. I can feel it.

12

UNEXPECTED

— PATRICK —

SEVERAL DAYS HAVE PASSED since my run-in with the bull, and with a hundred miles now behind us, Ted's departure is drawing near. Eight days into our adventure, my body is weary from constantly pushing, but I feel rejuvenated from the break we took yesterday in the small metropolis of Logroño. A day off from the trail offered time to stretch my muscles, rest my body, and take in the city's slow-paced culture. Much of our time was spent enjoying café con leches and Spanish tortillas for breakfast, and rich Tempranillo wine with paella for dinner in the courtyard at the center of the city.

Now on the trail, I can see Ted is beginning to move slower as his time here winds down. He has given 150 percent every step of the way in an effort to ensure that Justin and I have the greatest chance of success on this journey. Giving beyond what his body could reasonably do, I think he has hurt himself in the process. Even with a limp, Team Ted continues to help move us forward.

The seventeen miles from Logroño to Nájera are relatively uneventful. As we near our destination, we have the pleasure of meeting Carl and Deborah, two pilgrims in their late forties or early fifties whose journey has some obvious parallels to ours. Deborah has multiple sclerosis, and her small, frail body has suffered much from the disease. But she is mentally strong. As Carl cares for her, the love we see between them is astounding. Carl, who is tall and lean, has been walking nearby roads that parallel the Camino, while Deborah rolls alongside in her power wheelchair. They are only able to do segments of the trail where they can find places to recharge her wheelchair battery, but their commitment to each other and to the Camino is absolutely beautiful.

Watching Carl, I am reminded of Justin's wife, Kirstin, who bathes him, dresses him, and tends to his every need with a willing heart. Her background as a nurse has made the mechanics of caretaking easier, but the emotional strength required to care for someone you love is remarkable. Kirstin knew this was in her future when she married Justin, but she still said "I do." It's a brave and beautiful thing to give yourself to someone so completely.

After parting ways with Carl and Deborah, we continue on into town. As with so many of the quaint and beautiful towns we've been through, one night in Nájera doesn't seem nearly enough to appreciate the city for what it is. Still, after finding a place to rest our heads for the coming night, we drop off our backpacks and head out to explore as much as we can.

It isn't long before we happen upon a large courtyard surrounded by souvenir shops, bars, and restaurants. We couldn't care less about souvenirs, but a cold drink and dinner are high on our priority list. As we wait for our meals to be served, we find ourselves surrounded by a number of pilgrims we've met along the way, including Carl and Deborah. But there are also quite a few new faces.

I strike up a conversation with an American named Christie, who is sitting to my left at the end of a long string of tables. Her golden hair is pulled back in a ponytail, and her bright blue eyes match her inviting smile. Judging by her sun-kissed skin and strong, lean frame, she has spent a lot of time outdoors.

Christie has been walking the Camino with a friend, but her friend has suffered a foot injury and will be returning to the States in the morning. This means Christie will be walking the rest of the Camino alone.

As I enjoy my meal and give Justin bites of his paella—filled with chunks of chorizo, chicken, and shrimp—Christie asks about our Camino experience.

"We're headed all the way to Santiago—at least Justin and I are. Ted leaves in a few days."

"Doing this in a wheelchair is pretty crazy."

"Yeah, we get that a lot."

Soon, Ted and Justin join in, and we all have a lively conversation.

As we finish our meals, I turn to face Christie and ask, "What's your plan now that your friend is leaving?"

Before she can answer, Justin says, "You should join us tomorrow!"

Christie looks at the three of us and says, "Oh, I don't know. I think I'm going to go it alone for a while. I need to figure some things out."

She seems reluctant, so we don't press the issue, and after a while we head back to our rooms. Before we go, we tell Christie where we are staying and what time we're planning to leave, in case she changes her mind.

Back at the hotel, it's time for us to shower. Not many people find themselves giving their best friend a shower, but as I soap and rinse Justin, I'm reminded of Carl and of Kirstin. This is a privilege. It may be work at times; it may mean I'm the first one up in the morning and the last to bed, but to have the opportunity to tangibly express my love for my friend, to serve him, is a gift I cherish.

| | |

The first time I gave Justin a shower, I was visiting him in San Diego to give Kirstin a break from caring for their three kids and her husband while also working outside the home. It wasn't long after Justin had lost the use of his hands, so having others bathe him was still a relatively new experience.

The kids were in the living room while Justin and I went into the bathroom. As I helped him get undressed, he said, "I never thought I'd see the day when you would be taking my clothes off."

"Me neither."

As I wrapped my arms around him and lifted him onto the seat inside the shower, Justin laughed and said, "New territory for the both of us!"

In my years as a nurse, I've helped countless patients bathe, but this was very different.

"You're now officially the vice president of my inner circle," Justin said.

"What do you mean?"

"Kirstin's the president, and now you're vice president of my inner circle—the people who have had the pleasure of seeing me naked."

I just laughed, grabbed the spray nozzle, and began washing his hair.

| | |

— JUSTIN —

In the morning, the air is crisp and cool. While Patrick helps me get dressed, I sing a little song to him, as I have done every morning since Bayonne. Today's version goes like this:

> *There's Pat*
> *Puttin' on my socks*
> *Puttin' on my socks*
> *He's puttin' on my socks*

After three rounds of my spontaneous ditty, Patrick is smiling and laughing. If I can't dress myself, I will bring the comic relief.

Once I'm dressed, Ted bundles me up with my fleece jacket and fleece-lined chaps, which are like a miniature sleeping bag without a zipper. Ted drapes the chaps across my legs and tucks my feet into the pocket at the end. After securing the chaps around the leg rests of my wheelchair with one of the straps sewn into the fabric of the chaps, Patrick wraps a second strap around my waist to keep them from sliding down as we travel. We eat a quick breakfast at the hotel, but not before I find myself in time-out again. Before he grabs our food, Patrick realizes I'm facing a corner.

"Sorry about that, Skeez!" he says with a chuckle as he turns me around. I think he may have done it on purpose this time. After we enjoy some eggs and coffee, we're ready to get back on the trail.

As Ted washes down the last of his eggs with coffee, he looks at Patrick and then locks eyes with me.

"I don't like the thought of you guys being on your own."

As he stands to throw his backpack over his shoulder, he continues, "Tomorrow is my last day, and you guys are going to need some help."

With only a day and a half left with us before he has to fly home and return to work, the thought of Ted leaving gives us pause. Team Ted has been instrumental in getting us this far, but we have almost four weeks left on the trail before we reach Santiago.

Ted walks ahead of Patrick and opens the door so Patrick can push me outside. As we step into the chilly, early-morning air, the surrounding buildings cast lengthy shadows along the street. The one exception is a small park bench directly across from the hotel, bathed in brilliant sunlight streaming through a gap between the buildings.

Sitting on the bench is a young pilgrim with long blonde hair and a backpack resting at her feet. Bent over, she is cinching her hiking boots tight, but she raises her head when she hears us come outside. With a huge smile on her face, Christie is ready to push. Help has arrived.

Soon after we begin our walk, we are joined by John, a sixty-year-old retired US Naval officer and recycling specialist from San Diego, and Lynda, a young Canadian who teaches English at a school in Barcelona. Willing to lend a hand, they jump in to push or pull whenever necessary.

My backside is starting to get pretty sore again from the trail, and though my chair's shocks reduce the jarring of my bones,

I need another break from the rocky dirt path. Consulting our guidebook, we see that a highway, N-120, parallels the Camino for most of today's stretch to Santo Domingo de la Calzada. With this revised plan for the day, we work our way down a short stretch of trail to N-120.

As we set a comfortable pace along the paved roadway, Christie volunteers to push me so Patrick and Ted can just walk for a while. On the inclines, John and Lynda step in to help push and pull. For the first hour, the road is smooth and quiet. Pleased with our decision, my body is thanking us for the alternate route.

But not for long.

In our second hour of travel, traffic has increased dramatically. A multitude of cars, pickups, and semis are now speeding past us at seventy miles per hour, and we feel as if we're suddenly on the edge of a heavily traveled freeway. With no way to get off the road, we cross to the left-hand side, where at least we can see the traffic coming. Our situation now is anything but safe, and Patrick decides to move out front and start waving to get the attention of oncoming drivers. Most vehicles veer to the middle of the road to give us a few feet of room as they fly by, but some drivers insist on hugging the shoulder, missing us by a foot or so.

We soon learn from the film crew why so much traffic is barreling down a road that is supposed to be minimally traveled. A parallel freeway, A-20, is closed for construction, and every car, van, and truck has been diverted onto N-120, which is essentially a frontage road. With no way out of our current plight, we must simply make the best of the day. Christie, Ted, John, Lynda, and Patrick alternate between the jobs of pushing, pulling, and warning oncoming traffic.

Like so much of life, challenges come when you least expect them.

| | |

As I pulled into my driveway, the sky had already gone black, like a splash of ink backlit by a million tiny pinpricks of light. Inside our small turn-of-the-century home, my wife, Kirstin, and Jaden, our rambunctious toddler, had long since gone to bed. In our second year of parenting, we were still learning the ropes, and life had become even more chaotic when I launched my own graphic design business.

I shifted my green Toyota Tundra into park and killed the engine. When I stepped down onto the worn concrete pad, I used the side of the truck to steady myself as I worked my way around to the other side, one fragile step at a time, to where a short, curving walkway led up to the gated front porch.

The Southern California evening air was fresh and crisp—unusual for that time of year—and an eerie quiet hung over the neighborhood. Only the faint, distant hum of traffic challenged the occasional chirping of crickets, and a random scattering of porch lights pushed back against the night.

I lifted my right leg to step onto the raised walkway, but the six-inch riser proved too much and my legs folded underneath me. They had been getting weaker over the past few months, but this time it felt like someone had taken a baseball bat to the back of my knees. Going down hard and rolling onto my left shoulder, I was completely taken by surprise. I had become accustomed to stumbling or falling every now and then, but this was uncharted territory.

For months, the cane Patrick made for me and a pair of orthotic leg braces had provided enough support to keep me on my feet and mobile. But as I labored to get my legs underneath me on the walkway, I wasn't sure I could even get up again.

Justin and Patrick at high
school graduation (1993)

Childhood friends: (L to R)
Patrick, friend, Justin (1979)

THE EARLY YEARS

Reunited!
Home from
college at
Patrick's
house (1994)

Justin giving his best man's toast at Patrick and Donna's wedding (1997). He had the whole room laughing and may have told an embarrassing story or two.

GROWING IN LIFE TOGETHER

Patrick's turn as the best man, in Justin and Kirstin's wedding (2000)

Our friendship has always been defined by adventure. In 2001, we traveled with our wives to Europe (L to R: Donna, Patrick, Kirstin, Justin).

At the Skeesuck family cabin in Donnelly, Idaho, the weekend of the infamous "bat incident"

Patrick carrying Justin out of the warm Caribbean water in Ocho Rios, Jamaica (2007)

▷ Our first day on the Camino, we faced the challenge of the Pyrenees Mountains.

▽ Enjoying a brief moment of rest in the middle of the Pyrenees

▲ As if the steepness weren't challenging enough, we also encountered plenty of thick mud.

In Pamplona, discussing options with a local welder for repairing Justin's wheelchair

▲ Resting in Estella with Team Ted

At the top of Alto de Perdón (Hill of Forgiveness), outside of Pamplona, a monument dedicated to pilgrims

▼ Cruz de Ferro, a beautiful place to leave burdens behind

▼ A long, hot day in the Meseta!

THE JOURNEY CONTINUES . . .

▼ The steep climb up O Cebreiro with Joe out front

▲ We will never forget those we met on the Camino. Without the help of people like these, we would never have made it to Santiago!

▲ Patrick playing the guitar outside an albergue in Sarria

▲ Almost there! Looking at the city of Santiago de Compostela from the monument of Monte do Gozo

Brotherhood: Pursuing life with one another leads to amazing adventures. Justin and Patrick embracing a quiet moment together at the Samos Monastery.

Struggling to my feet and using my cane for balance, I managed to take a few more steps before I fell again—this time even harder. Twice now, in less than six feet, my body had hit the ground, and my legs felt weaker than ever.

Gathering my wits one more time and mustering all my strength, I slowly rose to my knees. Pulling on my cane for some semblance of leverage, I was able to get myself vertical again.

You can do this, I whispered under my breath, but I wasn't convinced by my words.

One more step and down I went again. Tears of anger, frustration, and pain welled up in my eyes and dampened my cheeks.

Fighting back the lump in my throat, I reached out, one arm at a time, and pushed up against the cool concrete beneath me, dragging myself the remaining twenty feet to the front porch.

Looking up at the weathered gray gate, I reached my arm around the corner of one of the pillars framing the entrance and heaved my body onto the stoop. Catching my breath, I looked out into the silent, dark night and tried to make sense of things.

This can't be happening. Not yet. I'm not ready for this.

Never had I felt more angry, broken, and alone.

| | |

— PATRICK —

With constant traffic speeding past us and everyone on high alert, Ted and I are second-guessing our decision to take the N-120 route. Even the slightest drift toward the roadway threatens Justin with severe injury—or worse. But with everyone working together, we proceed with caution, and several hours after what has proved to be one of the worst decisions of the trip, we arrive in the town of Santo Domingo de la Calzada.

With the dirt of the trail now under our feet, I am filled with relief, and my pulse slows as the stress of the day gradually recedes.

We stop at the first albergue we reach, but find the only beds available are on the second floor and there's no elevator. Though frustrating, this isn't something we can't overcome. We ask the woman behind the counter whether there are any albergues in town with beds on the first floor.

She shakes her head but directs us to one nearby that has an elevator. Rank with days of sweat, our clothes need laundering, and we're hungry after our long, stressful day. Justin opts for a nap, so I transfer him onto his bed for some shut-eye, while Ted and I hatch a plan to launder clothes and prepare dinner.

Because our albergue, like most, has a kitchen for pilgrims to use, we decide to cook tonight. While I find a small laundromat, Ted heads to the local *supermercado* to buy some food. When we return to our room, Justin is awake and ready for dinner. Dropping off our clean clothes, we load him into his chair and head to the kitchen.

As we join thirty pilgrims—including Carl and Deborah—from ten countries, the excitement is palpable. While Ted and I cook a simple dinner of spaghetti and sausage, Justin meets a multitude of new people. Stories and jokes are shared in multiple languages—with punch lines in English, Spanish, Italian, German, and Japanese. Bottles of wine are passed from pilgrim to pilgrim, the food is communal, and laughter is abundant. Seeing so many different cultures and so many walks of life represented, I can't help but smile.

I lean back in my seat and watch as people embrace the evening with joy and laughter. No one is left out, and everyone here is part of something bigger than themselves.

With bellies full and eyes heavy, we clean up our dishes and prepare to head back to our room. Justin wants to take a shower, but getting him into one is often difficult because of the size of his chair and the fact that he can't stand up. In Los Arcos, we borrowed a bistro chair, which we then used to carry Justin into the narrow shower stall. In Bayonne, we used a desk chair to get Justin into the bathroom, and I transferred him onto the toilet while I repositioned the chair inside the shower so that Justin would have something to sit on. Then I lifted him from the toilet onto the chair. We followed the same procedure in Estella, but there we had no choice but to use a leather chair. Our room tonight has a large enough shower, but nothing to sit on.

As we look for another chair to abuse, Justin says, "I would love to have just one shower where you didn't have to put me in a chair and drag me into the bathroom."

Carl overhears us discussing our game plan and says, "Hey guys, Deborah and I have an accessible room, and you're more than welcome to use the shower."

Justin looks at Carl and says, "Seriously?"

Carl just smiles and nods his head.

"That would be amazing!" Justin says.

Equipped with our tiny travel towels, soap, and a change of clothes, we make our way to the only accessible room we have seen in an albergue—and for the first time on our trip, a shower that has a place for Justin to sit. After I transfer him to a seat far more comfortable than a bistro chair, Justin asks if I can let him soak for a bit before washing him up. He makes the most of this opportunity and enjoys the warm, clean water.

Now showered and in bed, Justin is close to asleep, Ted is already snoring, and I begin getting ready for the morning.

Every night, I set out clothes for Justin to make the morning routine more efficient, check the wheelchair for any loose nuts and bolts, shower Justin when we have the opportunity, and take my own shower as well. Before the sun rises tomorrow, I'll be up first to get dressed and fill our water bottles and the reservoir in Justin's backpack. After brushing my teeth and making sure our bags are packed, I'll wake Justin, help him use his urinal, get him dressed—while enduring whatever song he has for me—transfer him from the bed to his chair, and brush his teeth, and we'll be off.

All this, in addition to each day's walking and pushing, is making me a kind of tired I didn't know existed. But tonight feels different. I have a sense of gratitude I haven't felt before. The challenge of the day with so much traffic, the fact of Ted leaving us tomorrow, and the communal dinner we experienced tonight have me thinking about what it means to face the challenges of life alone, to take on the unexpected in isolation. I wasn't designed for a solitary existence. Though I am so very tired, there is an underlying energy in my bones, an energy that comes from the presence and help of others.

The unexpected is just that—unexpected! We can't plan for it . . . we can't predict it . . . we can't be ready for it in any way. Often the unforeseen events in life come with few answers or no clear way out. Deborah's MS offers no way out, and Justin's disease will eventually take his life. But just like the highway, these unexpected challenges can be faced and life can be lived, despite the darkness. We just have to make sure we don't face them alone.

Ted has helped us get this far. Christie, Lynda, and John have offered to help in the coming days. The many pilgrims sitting, breaking bread, and enjoying wine tonight remind me of what the church is supposed to mean, what it is supposed to represent. We are a community—or at least we should be—where all are welcome, all are loved, and the unexpected challenges of life are faced with others at our side.

13

THE LIES WE TELL OURSELVES

— JUSTIN —

TODAY IS AN EMOTIONAL DAY. As Patrick and I head toward Belorado, accompanied by our new friends Christie, John, and Lynda, Team Ted is getting ready to return to Idaho—and just in time. Over the past forty-eight hours, his limp has increased, and he is visibly in pain. Even so, Patrick and I are reluctant to see him go. Ted has been instrumental to our journey in so many ways. With his impending departure, we realize how much he has sacrificed to help us when we needed it most.

The past ten days have been filled with so many memories—the mud and false summits in the Pyrenees, the broken wheel in Pamplona, Patrick checking out a man in a dress, traversing poppy fields, running with bulls, eating dinner with the other pilgrims. Ted helped create each of these memories. Starting today, every Camino story will be one that Ted isn't a part of. This is tough to swallow. But though he may not be with us from here until the end, the days up until now have made every day in the future possible. I suppose life is this way. The events of our past and the relationships that have gone before make new things possible, good or bad.

Ted starts the day walking with us for one last stretch of the Camino, but after a few hours, his part of the journey has officially come to an end. When Robin finds an access point where he can get his car close to the trail, we all stop for a round of good-byes.

Patrick locks the brakes to my chair, unclips from the harness behind me, and gives Ted a bear hug filled with more gratitude than any words could ever express.

"Thank you! Thank you so much for everything you've done."

Releasing Patrick, Ted smiles. "You bet!"

He then comes over to me and bends down to wrap his arms around my shoulders. I often miss being able to return hugs, but never more than I do right now.

"Love you, brother," I whisper to him.

As he walks toward the car, he turns to face us. "Love you guys. Thanks for letting me be a part of this."

With one last wave to everyone in the group, Ted crawls into Robin's car with his backpack and is on his way to the airport.

The dynamic of our group has suddenly shifted. One of the most familiar faces in our lives is gone, and we're now accompanied by three people we hardly know. But there is a certain mystery to the Camino, one that often turns complete strangers into friends by the end of the day.

The combination of being completely unplugged from the stresses of work, computers, and phones causes some kind of mental reboot. With no meetings, no projects, and no commitments, people tend to open up and provide details of their lives you wouldn't normally expect to hear after just meeting. Eight hours of walking together provides ample time for sharing.

In addition to the abundance of quality time and minimal distractions, people on the Camino tend to be seekers of openness and honesty. They embrace a community in which relationships are treasured. This is an environment where pilgrims feel safe. For some reason, Christie has found that safe place with me.

"So, Christie, tell me about yourself," I say as she begins pushing me down the trail.

"Umm . . . uh . . . I don't know where to start," she stammers.

After a moment of thought, she decides to start at the beginning, zeroing in on the darkest and most painful moments of her childhood. This soon leads to stories of self-destructive tendencies. As a young girl, she struggled with crippling fears and insecurities and developed an eating disorder. She suffered temptations toward self-harm and became suicidal. Over time, Christie allowed her identity to be swallowed by the darkest experiences of her childhood. She could only see herself through the lenses of her depression, fears, and insecurities. She believed so many lies about who she was and who she is that she couldn't see through them to recognize the amazing God-breathed creation she was meant to be.

"For the first time, I am beginning to see there is more to me than my past," she says as she continues to push me. "I think I'm here to let go of a lot of my darkness.

"For years, I have locked away the pain; but here on the Camino I'm learning to tell a different story. These horrible things may have happened to me, but they will not define me!"

As Christie continues to push me at a steady rate, I tell her, "You're right! The past doesn't have to define us, but we can't face it alone."

| | |

— PATRICK —

Listening to Christie's openness and honesty with Justin, I am flooded with memories of my own self-destructive tendencies.

I had a very privileged childhood. We were never wealthy—in fact, we were quite poor—but my sister and brothers and I were always loved, taken care of, and never went hungry. Justin and his brother and sister grew up in similar circumstances—our homes were safe places and our parents set a good example for us. Unfortunately, this didn't mean I was immune to the world's destructive forces.

Every child is bound to have a brush with some form of pain, whether initiated by an outside force, such as abuse or neglect, or by some other unhealthy choice. We all, at some point, have made decisions that negatively impact us. For me, this started very young.

The first time I saw a picture of a naked woman, I was seven years old. I was playing in the backyard at a friend's house when we heard the sound of his dad's car pulling out of the garage. As his dad drove away, my friend asked me if he could show me a secret. Intrigued, I followed him inside. We walked up the stairs to his parents' room, and he slid open a closet door. Inside, we found his dad's collection of *Playboy* and *Penthouse* magazines. There were stacks of literally hundreds of them, many dating back to the 1970s.

Eyes wide with curiosity, I began to thumb through the images. Not knowing what to expect, my curiosity soon became insatiable. A sense of guilt washed over me, but that was quickly stifled by a more powerful draw—what comes next?

Over the next several months, my friend and I kept track of which magazines we had looked through so we could get to the ones we had yet to see. This exploration of the female anatomy continued off and on over the next several years. By the time I was nine, some of the images in the newer magazines depicted explicit sex. Nothing was left to the imagination.

My initial curiosity wasn't sexual in nature—after all, I was only seven—but by the time I was in middle school, I thought about pornography constantly. My ideas of what a man and a woman should be to one another, how they should treat each other, had been heavily influenced by the love and respect my parents showed each other, but a dark and deceptive voice was growing louder.

When I was thirteen, I smoked marijuana and drank alcohol for the first time. I enjoyed the way they both made me feel. My mind felt free and boundless each time I got high. Often when I wasn't with Justin, I would go for walks to smoke a joint or I would seek out parties or gatherings where weed and booze were likely to be available. Sometimes these parties included pornographic movies. By the time I was in high school, I had a few adult films on VHS stashed away in my bedroom under my mattress or at the back of one of my drawers. They often sat next to a bag of green buds waiting to be rolled into joints or stuffed into a bong. I found ways to get high as often as I could, and eventually I struck a deal with a few guys in town to deliver weed for them in exchange for a free supply for myself. I experimented with other drugs, but marijuana was always my first choice.

Throughout high school, I often had some weed in my possession, and though Justin knew about my drug use, I rarely did anything around him. Not because he looked down on me, but he was just never particularly drawn to it himself. Pornography, however, was another story.

| | |

— JUSTIN —

Second grade should be a time when kids learn how to write stories and master addition and subtraction, rather than being exposed to pornography. I was a smart kid and had no problem with second grade math or writing, but my mind was often filled with images of naked women. A boy in my class had stolen a magazine from his dad's collection, and our curiosity about the female body drove us to peruse the images with some frequency.

Though it seemed innocuous at first, and my understanding of what I was seeing was limited, a quiet longing to see more was growing in my mind. With the turn of each page, I became more thoroughly intoxicated by the airbrushed beauty depicted there. By the time I turned twelve, I had a pocket calendar of topless women hidden in my room. But that wasn't enough. I felt a growing desire to see more—a hunger that was hard to explain and even harder to satisfy.

By early high school, what I was seeing in those explicit magazines was undermining what my parents had taught me about how women should be treated and respected. Every picture and every lustful thought polluted my view of my female friends, fellow students, and later, my coworkers. I explained away my compulsive desire, telling myself, *It's okay; it's human nature to be attracted*. But in convincing myself that what I was experiencing was normal, I was giving the secret I carried more weight and more control.

Every time I sought to satisfy my "need," I could feel the grip of pornography tightening. The tighter the grip, the darker the secret; the darker the secret, the more power my addiction had over me, and the greater my need. For years, both Patrick and I struggled with this addiction independently.

We were in college before we knew about each other's struggle, and it would be several more years before we reached the level of honesty and vulnerability we are experiencing here on the Camino. Christie's struggles may differ—the lies she's believed are not the same ones I've believed—but I see a common thread. Christie, Patrick, and I have all exchanged truth for lies. Christie is walking into this realization afresh.

| | |

— PATRICK —

With the sun high above us, I am now pushing Justin, and Christie is walking alongside. We continue our conversation, exploring questions of self-worth and our thoughts on overcoming the struggles of life. We all agree that we must embrace the truth that no matter what we have done or what has been done to us, we all have value and can choose to be a part of creating a community that offers safety and love.

Turning to Justin, Christie asks, "Do you think there's a difference between this kind of community and church?"

Justin mulls over her question before answering.

"Community like this is what church was meant to be, what it should be," Justin says. "But unfortunately, it is often not what the church *is*."

"What does 'church' mean to you, Patrick?" Christie asks.

If I'm honest with myself, church is what we have been experiencing for the past several miles, but how do I best express this?

"I think I want to start with what it's not," I say.

As I pause to gather my thoughts, the sound of our steps seems to drive the words into my mouth.

"Church is not a building for worship or a place to learn theories about religious doctrine. It's not about why 'we' are right and 'they' are wrong, or how to talk to 'those people.'"

"Okay, so what is it then?"

"It is an existence grounded in loving God and loving others—regardless of race, creed, sexual preference, or one's history of pain, abuse, or addiction—and drawing them into the truth."

"What truth?" she asks.

"The truth that God's love is more powerful than any darkness we can face."

Jesus painted a picture, time and time again, of a group of individuals in community with one another, living life together, facing the problems of the world together, loving together without an agenda, and putting the needs of others above their own. For many, myself included, church has been reduced to a place to go for a couple of hours on Sunday morning, instead of being a vibrant community of people committed to living life together, committed to loving one another. But here on the Camino, I am discovering a new appreciation for a different kind of church—the church Jesus called us to *live*, not one we simply attend.

Don't get me wrong, I find value in "going to church," but I often feel as if the church has been reduced to a club with exceptionally high acceptance standards, where everyone who is a member has been forced to lie on their application just to get in. Too often, I've seen a refusal to be real with one another and to invite others into our pain because we are afraid we won't meet the criteria—criteria created by man, not by God. So many people today "do church" by going through the motions and checking the boxes. As a result, religion takes precedence over relationship. Here with Christie, relationship is in the driver's seat, and her openness reminds me of the beauty that exists when love is lived out.

Jesus calls us to live this way, to live in relationship with one another, to live in community with one another—a community the apostle Paul has a few choice words to say about in 1 Corinthians 13, often referred to as "the love chapter."

> Love never gives up. Love cares more for others than it does for itself. Love is not proud or boastful, and does not force itself on others. Love is slow to anger and does not keep score of the sins of others. Love does not take joy in the suffering of others. Love finds pleasure in the truth.[1]

Quite simply, this is how we are supposed to live our lives. The result is a community where all feel welcome and safe; a place where healing can occur; an existence we are all called to live.

Christie's openness and vulnerability remind me of a lesson I learned at an age much older than hers. Her pain, guilt, and suffering wielded incredible controlling power over her while it was kept secret. Each time she shares her story, though, a little more light shines inside the closet where her skeletons reside. The more light she lets in, the fewer shadows there are for those skeletons to hide within. Eventually, the light will become so strong, so intense, that those skeletons will be reduced to ash.

What Christie experienced as a child will never be miraculously taken away, but the power those experiences have over her is being transferred into her hands. She is choosing how those memories, combined with all the life she has lived since, will become a part of her identity.

Have I taken control of my own darkness? My porn addiction and drug use are not things I'm proud of, but I don't shy away from their existence, at least not anymore. For years, I stuffed the guilt and shame away in my own closet. But the more I kept these things hidden, the stronger they became. Pornography, in particular, drew me deeper into depravity, enveloping my every waking thought. I would try to fight the addiction alone, and I would win . . . for a while. But it always came back, and when it did, it was stronger than before.

For the longest time, I would be honest about what I was doing and what I was seeing, but only when I was caught. I guess that isn't really being honest. But when I began to tell others about my addiction, the control seemed to loosen its grip, and the weight of the load I was carrying became a little lighter.

I invited my wife into that conversation. I invited Justin into that conversation, and now I am inviting Christie into that conversation, the way she has invited us into her story. As a result, I find freedom in their knowing all of me and still choosing to love me.

It wasn't easy; I was fearful and worried that others might judge me and think less of me, or cast me aside as unworthy. But the opposite happened. When I shared with those whom I trusted, with those who made me feel safe, I realized I wasn't alone. We all struggle; we all have some form of darkness in our lives—past or present. But even though these shadows or stains are a part of our story, they don't have to define us.

When we invite others into our world, when we surround ourselves with a community of trusted individuals, we are able to share like Christie has been sharing. And we begin to realize we're not alone in our suffering, and we're not alone in life. Our stories begin to take on a different shape; they're filled with hope. Soon, the beauty of our relationships outweighs the darkness of our pasts, and people—like Ted and Christie—can help us create new memories as we continue to write our stories.

The Camino is filled with people who are dealing with something—searching for a safe place to face their demons. How different would the world be if every church offered that safe place?

14

THE RIDICULOUS
AND THE ABSURD

— JUSTIN —

THOUGH PATRICK DOES most of the pushing, Christie, John, and Lynda put in their fair share of work as well. In fact, Christie has earned the nickname "Mini-Ted." Though only a fraction of Ted's size, she is a true workhorse. Whenever Patrick struggles with the long inclines, she straps in without hesitation and pulls like an ox. Both John and Lynda have eagerly provided help as well. We didn't ask for their assistance, but they continue to freely give it; it is beautiful.

I continue to find it humbling when someone offers help, and I have tried to make it a habit to always accept. Patrick and my wife might disagree, because of my stubborn streak. When my hands started to go, I still insisted on tying my own shoes, even when someone offered. In fact, I continued to tie them—no matter how long it took me—until I literally could no longer do it. It was the same with brushing my teeth and using the bathroom. So yeah, I'm a little stubborn. Out here, though, stubbornness is of no use to me. I am completely at the mercy of others. Without my power wheelchair, my opportunities to demonstrate independence are nil, so I embrace any help offered.

When Patrick doesn't need help pushing or pulling, our three new friends walk beside us in conversation. Sometimes these conversations are very serious, sometimes silly and awkward.

As we work our way down the trail, John shouts out, "Does this backpack make my butt look big?"

Christie just rolls her eyes and says, "Are you sure you want me to answer that?"

Each day brings us all a little closer as friends and fellow pilgrims. Just as navigating the struggles of life together helps facilitate a strong bond between people, so do the moments when we can laugh with—and sometimes at—one another. Patrick and I have had plenty of these moments.

We arrive in the town of San Juan de Ortega in the early afternoon. This particular town boasts a thriving population of eighteen, complete with one albergue, one church, and one small hotel. Patrick and I opt for a room at the hotel because Patrick's back is wearing down from too many nights on paperthin albergue mattresses. Also, most of the albergues have bunk beds, and there's no way to get me into a top bunk. Patrick has often had to transfer me into the bottom bunk, which is usually no more than eighteen inches off the ground. Lifting 200 pounds in and out of a bed this low, while trying to avoid knocking his head on the upper bunk, has taken its toll.

After dropping off our bags at the hotel, we head over to the albergue, which is the only place in town where we can get food. Mike, Robin, Terry, and Jasper are already there, enjoying the warm sun and a reprieve from the day's work. Patrick and I find a shady spot and capitalize on the opportunity to relax.

With his feet up on a chair in front of him, Patrick alternates between lifting a glass of cold beer to my lips and taking sips of his own.

Over the years, Patrick has perfected the art of feeding me and giving me a drink whenever a straw is not available. By trial and error, he has learned how much food I can take in one bite, and when he lifts a glass to my lips, I give a slight nod to let him know when I'm done.

For the most part, it works pretty well, and we're both able to finish our meals at about the same time. But sometimes there are a few hang-ups—such as right now, when Patrick is spending more time drinking and talking with our fellow pilgrims and less time giving me a hand.

Not wanting to bite the hand that feeds me, I try to be patient throughout the process, but after an hour or so, his glass is empty and mine is still half full.

When he turns back toward me again, I raise my eyebrows in mock disdain for his neglect. But I can't hold the pose for long, and I start to laugh.

"Just giving you a hard time, but could I have the rest of my beer?"

Chuckling, he lifts my glass and pretends to drink it, but then he holds it to my lips so I can enjoy the cool liquid as it counters the heat of the day. While I drink, he says, "Sorry about that."

When it's time for dinner, Patrick, Terry, and I head into the bar adjacent to the albergue. In these small Spanish towns, the bars are the center of commerce, places where you can find a meal, buy a few provisions, and even find, from time to time, an ice cream cone. We order a few bocadillos, take our food to a table, and settle in to enjoy our meal. These simple sandwiches of cured ham, cheese, and rustic bread have been a staple since we began this journey.

As the three of us wrap up our dinner, we enjoy some quiet conversation. "Do you want anything for dessert?" Patrick asks me.

"You know me. I'll do anything for something that ends in *ocolate*!"

A number of people have been ordering food at the counter to my left, and I notice an unkempt woman in her fifties who stands five-foot-nothing but clearly has some spunk. With her long, tangled, dark brown hair pulled back in a ponytail, and her wide-eyed look, she aggressively orders something from the counter, punctuating her words with wild hand gestures and almost maniacal laughter.

Turning from the counter with a chocolate-and-nut-covered ice cream cone in hand, she immediately locks eyes with me as she takes the first few bites.

Something is about to go down; I can feel it.

Without breaking eye contact, she walks directly toward me and begins peppering me with staccato Spanish. I speak enough Spanish to get by, but she's talking way too fast for me to keep up. Nevertheless, the confused smile on my face seems to tell her I understand every word.

After taking a few more bites of her ice cream cone, she smiles, rattles off a few more Spanish words, and shoves the half-eaten cone into my mouth. I don't even get an opinion in the matter. I'm going to share with her whether I like it or not.

Meanwhile, Patrick, my guardian and protector, is just sitting there watching it all unfold.

"Aren't you going to do something?" I ask him with a laugh.

He just shakes his head and says, "Nope!"

Smiling, I say, "I guess I *will* do anything for something that ends in *ocolate*."

Patrick then reaches across the table and grabs my phone to take a picture.

Both he and Terry are laughing hysterically as the woman alternates between putting the cone in her own mouth and then into mine. It's one thing to have someone like Patrick feed me food I've ordered. But having a complete stranger force-feed me ice cream I didn't ask for? This is strange, to say the least. The truth is, I feel a little violated. For the record, if you want to help someone in a wheelchair, a good rule of thumb is to ask first.

But this gal is bright and joyful with each bite she crams into my face. She clearly thinks she is giving me a wonderful gift, so I decide to embrace it. This is definitely a first for me. But truth be told, if the tables were turned and Patrick were the one sitting in a wheelchair, I would have done the exact same thing—watch and laugh.

| | |

Though Patrick is getting the best of me here, I've had plenty of opportunities to laugh at him as well, much the same way he and Terry are laughing at me now.

During our senior year of high school, I worked on the yearbook, which often meant taking photos at school events. In the spring, Patrick was nominated to the homecoming court, and there was an assembly scheduled to announce the king and queen. On the day of the event, I was in the gymnasium, sitting at the base of the bleachers with several friends and family members of the nominees, while most students were still in their classrooms awaiting release for the assembly.

The previous year's prom was the first time Patrick had worn a tux, and he and I had opted for vests. But for the homecoming court, all the young men were wearing cummerbunds. I didn't know it at the time, but Patrick was in the back room struggling to get his shirt flat and smooth so his cummerbund would lie properly across his stomach. His limited experience with tuxedos meant he was unaware of the holes inside his pants pockets that provide access to keep shirts straight and taut. Patrick's solution was to reach in through his fly. Shortly after he adjusted his shirt, he was asked by one of the teachers to take some papers to me before the students showed up.

Sitting on the edge of the front row of bleachers with camera in hand, I could see Patrick walking toward me with his tuxedo jacket on, cummerbund nice and flat, shoes polished to a brilliant shine, and about five inches of stark white dress shirt sticking out of his open zipper. I had three options: I could take a picture and immortalize the moment; quickly come to his rescue; or embarrass him in front of everyone else who was sitting there. We are best friends, after all. Option three seemed the only logical choice.

As I stood up and walked toward Patrick, he was still absolutely clueless to the white Pinocchio nose sticking straight out of the front of his pants. As he handed me the papers, I quickly put them in the pocket of my shorts, grabbed the front of his pants, and stuffed his shirt back into his fly. The mortified look on his face was priceless. He just stood there in a mild form of shock, so I zipped up his fly and leaned forward to whisper in his ear, "If you want your shirt to be flat, use the holes in the pockets of your pants. That's what they're for." Speechless, he turned around to go back to the waiting area.

"Go get 'em, Paddy!" I said as I smacked him on the butt.

Returning to my seat, I could tell by the smiles and laughter coming from the people waiting for the assembly that I had made the right decision.

| | |

— PATRICK —

In my relationship with Justin, turnabout is fair play.

As a soccer player, he wore Umbro shorts on and off the field. The lightweight nylon provided plenty of mobility and freedom on the field, and the shorts were incredibly comfortable to wear day to day.

Near the end of our senior year, the day arrived for our school-sanctioned "senior skip day," and our class decided to drive three and a half hours up to Wallowa Lake, Oregon, a small mountain resort where my family often vacationed in the summer months. The lake water is cold in late May, but the air temperature is warm enough for swimming, and there are several miniature golf courses, coffee and ice cream shops, and ample hiking trails in the area, which meant we had plenty of activities to occupy ourselves for most of the day.

Late in the afternoon, Justin, our friend Chris, and I were sitting on the docks chatting with a group of girls.

With the sun shining down on us from the west and shadows growing taller behind us, we enjoyed the light's reflection as it danced across the surface of the water. Surrounding mountain peaks looked back at us from their mirrorlike images reflecting off the face of the lake, and the scent of pine trees filled the air. Surrounded by God's incredible creation and good friends, how could this moment have been any better?

Justin was sitting on the dock with his legs in a V, basking in the sun as we talked with our lady friends. I had been sitting behind him in the full sun, but had grown tired of the heat, so I stood up to move to the edge of the dock, where I could put my feet in the water. As I stepped around Justin, I noticed that his Umbros had ridden up and that the boxers he was wearing underneath were not performing their intended function.

This presented a bit of a conundrum. Should I get Justin's attention to warn him that he was about to experience sunburn in a place that should never see the light of day? Did I risk embarrassing him in front of the girls? Or was it a moot point since he had been sitting like this for a good half hour? Surely the girls would have noticed and were just too polite to point out what was painfully obvious to all but Justin.

I sat quietly until the girls moved on to some other activity. As soon as they were out of earshot, I walked over to Justin, leaned down, and said, "Hey Skeez, Umbros and boxers don't mix."

At first, Justin looked at me in confusion, but then he glanced down at his shorts.

"Dude! Why didn't you tell me! Do you think they noticed?"

"I don't know how they couldn't have."

— JUSTIN —

Patrick and I are firm believers that humor and laughter are as important to our friendship as openness and honesty about the struggles we face. Here on the Camino, we've overcome obstacles, fear, and doubt because of the strength and love we freely give each other. We've built relationships along the way by inviting others into our vulnerability and honesty. But our ability to laugh at each other, to laugh together, and to share the hilarity of our friendship has given us extra fuel on this journey. A bond forged through laughter—a bond that cannot be broken—lightens our load.

15

MUCH-NEEDED REST

— JUSTIN —

I'M TIRED, AND PATRICK IS EXHAUSTED. Our rest day in Logroño feels like it was more than just five days ago. Since then, we've averaged fifteen miles a day, and we have one more day of walking before our next planned off day, in the city of Burgos. We're ready for some respite from the grind of day in, day out walking. The trek from San Juan de Ortega to Burgos proves difficult, and the trail is rocky and incredibly uneven. Patrick is forced to zigzag along the trail in order to find enough even ground to navigate without jarring me too much in the wheelchair. Cresting a hill on the trail outside of Burgos with John, Christie, and Lynda at our sides, we encounter an even taller ascent littered with many large stones sticking up from the dirt. Some are as tall as eighteen inches. These stones make it impossible for the wheels of my chair to continue to roll forward.

Patrick and I discuss our options to get beyond this section, and only one solution seems possible: I'll have to be carried. We consider using the sling like we did on the Pyrenees, but without Ted to assist, we're not sure we can do it. Although we're surrounded by people who are willing to help, we're not sure that anyone is strong enough or tall enough to keep my back and butt from hitting the protruding rocks below. Additionally, there is no safe place to set me down while those who carry me rest their backs and arms.

"What do you think about just trying to carry the whole chair with Justin in it?" Christie asks. This seems to be our best option, but with a combined weight of 250 pounds, it will be no easy feat.

Bernie from Ireland joined us a few days ago, which gives us a team of five, but as they try to hoist my chair over the stones and boulders, it quickly becomes clear we need another person to even out the load. As we discuss what to do next, a muscular man in his midfifties walks past us up the hill with a confident stride. When he reaches the top, he drops his backpack on the ground and turns to jog back down. As he approaches us, he barks out in a thick Australian accent, "You're going to need help. What can I do?"

Patrick smiles and says, "Can you give us a hand carrying the wheelchair up the hill?"

The man nods in agreement, and we are grateful for his assistance.

Before he grabs the side of my chair, the man rests a reassuring hand on my shoulder and says, "My name's Ray, and I'm retired from the Australian Special Forces. The Yanks helped me out so much in Vietnam, this is the least I can do."

With Ray, we now have six sets of hands. Patrick and Christie hoist up the handlebars in the back and use their shoulders for leverage, while Ray and Lynda grab the aluminum rails on each side of my chair, and John and Bernie lift the footrest. It's a constant struggle to find secure footing while keeping the welded front wheel from bashing against the rocks, but the crew manages through the rough terrain. For several hundred feet, they haul me toward the top of the next hill, while keeping up a constant dialogue among themselves.

"Watch your step."

"Rock to your right."

"Careful, that one's loose."

The uneven terrain means I'm never level. Though my friends do their best to keep me from tipping over, I feel the strain of the seat belt across my lap as it holds me in place.

"You guys got this!" I shout.

Finally, we make it the top, but even with all the help, this last section has been especially taxing, and Patrick and I are increasingly weary.

We have been away from home for three weeks and have traveled nearly 180 miles in twelve days on the trail. We're grateful for all the help we've received along the way—starting with Team Ted and continuing with Christie, Lynda, John, Bernie, and now Ray (not to mention the many other volunteers who have stepped in from time to time)—but the trail has taken its toll, and we desperately need tomorrow's day of rest. We work our way toward the city of Burgos while the others either walk ahead or fall behind. Patrick and I move quietly together in silence as we enter town. We find our hotel, check in, and get settled. With backpacks off and feet bare, we lie down to take a nap.

Lying on my back, with my chair resting beside me, I can hear Patrick's slow and steady breathing from the bed next to mine. I'm tired, but my mind is full and sleep eludes me.

For the past eighteen days, Patrick and I have been together almost every waking moment. During the day we've had every meal together, and have taken every step and every roll of the wheels together. At night, we are always in the same room. Well over a third of the way through the Camino, with about three hundred miles to go, we haven't had a single disagreement. Even with the many struggles we've faced—the Pyrenees, the broken wheel, the wear on both our bodies, the hill we've just come over—we haven't had one fight about directions, or how to navigate an obstacle, or when to leave town each morning. With our two strong wills, I think we both expected some conflict by now. But there hasn't been any, at least not between us.

Several times before we left on this journey, we were told how unique our friendship is. Since being on the trail, we've heard others say the same thing.

When we first met Christie, she told us, "I've never seen a friendship like this before." And even though Ted knows both of us, he made a similar comment right before he left. I can't help but wonder why what we have is so rare.

As kids, we didn't know our friendship was unique. It's just the way it's always been—and maybe we've taken it for granted. But why are strong friendships so uncommon? Certainly, the chemistry between us is based on a lot of shared experiences, but is there something else we've done that makes our level of connection possible?

When Patrick gets up from his nap, we make a plan to tend to our laundry so we can wear clean clothes tomorrow. Patrick has periodically washed our underwear and socks in sinks or showers with the hopes of minimizing our stench, but his efforts are no match for a washing machine. With a backpack full of filthy clothes, we head out to find a Laundromat.

Sitting outside the muggy room that houses four small

washers and dryers, we rest in each other's company—sometimes talking, sometimes saying nothing at all. There are no awkward pauses, and any lull in conversation feels natural. Silence is okay. In fact, it is more than okay; it is welcomed. We welcome the silence—not because we need a break from each other's words, but because in some strange way, the silence we share is ours. It's a time of comfort and rest—our comfort and rest.

After Patrick finishes with the clothes, he stuffs them back into his backpack and we return to our room. We speak little, other than to discuss a plan for dinner. We've been surviving on traditional pilgrim meals—including hearty potato-and-onion omelets known as *tortillas españolas* for breakfast, and bocadillos for lunch—but the variety has been lacking. Even though many restaurants have a pilgrim's menu, with dinners that are quite substantial and filling, tonight we opt for pizza.

As we enter a small pizza shop, Patrick is so focused on getting us food that he forgets he is pushing a wheelchair and not a shopping cart. He parks my chair in a corner and heads to the counter.

Looking over my shoulder, I shout, "Dude! Timeout?"

"Crap!"

He walks back to me, turns me around, and then returns to the counter to place our order. While standing in line, he hangs his head in shame. I know he is focused on managing everything for two, but I do get a kick out of giving him a hard time. It's what friends do.

When the pizza arrives, we enjoy our dinner, and the topic of tomorrow's day of rest rules the conversation.

Rest . . . Sabbath.

In the Christian tradition, the word *Sabbath*, or a day of rest, has usually been associated with the day people go to church or abstain from work, but it doesn't have to be reserved for Sundays. Right now, we need a day to rejuvenate, to appreciate what we have, and to reflect on this trip and the things we hold dear. It's easy to get caught up in the go, go, go of life—but not so much on the Camino. Our quiet moments sitting outside a Laundromat, and this dinner discussing our rest-day plans, have me thinking that just maybe this is one of the secrets to our friendship—the concept of Sabbath. It has clearly helped us enjoy the constant time spent in close proximity, but I think it may also have been a piece of what helped us endure so many years apart.

| | |

— PATRICK —

Spring of 1993 brought the end of our high school careers. Graduation came and went, and the stress of finishing high school was replaced by the anxiety of paying college tuition. Justin and I both qualified for a number of loans and scholarships, but they covered only a fraction of the cost of school. We both turned our focus to making money to pay for the remainder. While I swung a hammer for a construction company, building onion sheds on local farms, Justin was breaking the ground with shovels and pickaxes as he dug swimming pools in the backyards of neighborhood homes.

The work was grueling for both of us. Baking in the sun for eight to ten hours a day of manual labor drove a good work ethic into our brains and our bones, but by the end of a long Monday, we were already exhausted, and by the time Friday rolled around, we were desperate for a break from the heat, sweat, and sore muscles. If Justin's weakness was progressing, I couldn't tell. His leg brace offered enough support for him to manage the digging, and he had no problem driving to and from work.

We still found time to be together on the weekends, and the less time we had, the more precious it seemed. August was coming quickly, and Justin would soon be off to San Diego and Point Loma Nazarene College while I would head east to Northwest Nazarene College in Nampa.

The impending separation worried me, and I think Justin had his reservations as well. How would we stay connected? What would this time apart do to our relationship? With each passing weekend, we avoided focusing on the coming changes and embraced the time we had together. Even as teenagers, we had developed an appreciation for being present in the moment instead of worrying about what might come. Evenings were spent playing basketball, watching movies, or lying on our backs in one of our bedrooms listening to Pearl Jam's first album, *Ten*.

The day finally came for Justin to leave for California. After loading up his green Honda Accord, he gave me a hug.

"See you at Christmas?" he said.

"See you at Christmas."

As he drove away, I felt an emptiness that lasted for days—and seemed even heavier when I packed my belongings into my parents' car and headed to Nampa.

College life meant new friends, new activities, and new interests, but Justin and I made a point of calling each other every few weeks in an effort to stay connected. In the days before cell phones, when we had to consider the cost of long-distance charges whenever we picked up the phone, we somehow always had enough money to make the call—and those phone calls are fond memories for both of us. We rested in the company of each other's voice as we talked about school and girls. Other times, we sat in silence, knowing our best friend was on the other end of the line. Anytime there was a change, Justin would update me on his disease.

I still remember the day he told me things were getting worse.

"I've been getting some twitching in my upper calf, and when I'm not wearing my brace, I have to steady myself against a wall or a piece of furniture."

"What do the doctors say?" I asked.

"They're stumped."

"Is it still just your leg? Any chance of it spreading?"

"Nobody knows."

He told me about the many office visits, MRIs, and blood tests, and the painful muscle biopsies that hadn't yielded any results that would help with a diagnosis. Still, Justin remained positive in spite of it all—even when playing tennis grew more difficult.

By Christmas break, Justin's disease had progressed to the point that he had to give up playing tennis altogether. Though it still affected only his left leg, he was too unstable to run. When he came up to Nampa for a visit, I could see his gait had slowed and he now had to swing his weaker leg forward to compensate for his limp. More weakness and still no answers from the doctors.

Although his days of playing tennis and soccer had come to an end, he never dwelled on the loss. Instead he turned to new interests to invest his time and energy in. He learned to play guitar and poured many hours into watercolor and graphic design.

The following spring break was the first time Donna met Justin, and she was surprised to see his braces and his limited mobility. He now had to be careful on uneven terrain or when stepping down from a curb. I had told Donna stories about our boyhood mischief and how we loved spending time together, but I had failed to mention how Justin's disease was spreading. I hadn't omitted it intentionally . . . it just wasn't how I saw him.

During Justin's visit, we spent the warm spring afternoons and cool evenings listening to him explain his new art projects and the music scene in San Diego, and I fulfilled my role as the math and science nerd, explaining the new discoveries I was making in my classes. As we talked, Donna and Justin got to know each other, and I received his official stamp of approval for dating Donna.

Though it was challenging to maintain a close relationship while separated by a thousand miles, time and distance did little to diminish our friendship during our college years.

| | |

— JUSTIN —

The day after our arrival in Burgos, Patrick and I wander through the city, taking in the sights, sounds, and smells. We're captivated by the architecture of the four- and five-story buildings bordering the brick-paved Plaza Mayor. Each set of windows or doors boasts Juliet balconies, small patios with black wrought-iron railings. The buildings are painted different shades of yellow, pink, or white, and no two adjacent buildings are the same color. The pastel hues offer a stark contrast to the bright blue sky. We pass a small bakery, and the aroma of fresh-baked bread and warm pastries washes over us. Ambling through side streets and plazas, we eventually find ourselves at the base of the magnificent Cathedral of Saint Mary. We're intrigued by the ornate Gothic exterior, and the inside of this cathedral is even more stunning and awe inspiring.

While we admire some artwork in a glass enclosure, we are amazed at how quiet the cathedral is. Everyone steps softly as they take in the stained glass and carvings, and all we hear are hushed whispers.

"Hey! Aren't you Justin and Patrick?" A booming voice from across the room shatters the worshipful silence.

"Uh . . . yes," we both reply as two young men in their mid-twenties approach us.

"Hi, I'm Joe, and this is my buddy Richard. We're from Boise."

Halfway across the world and we run into two guys from our neck of the woods! Boise is only ten miles from our homes in Meridian.

"We've been following you guys on Facebook," Joe continues, "but this is pretty cool that our Camino actually crosses with yours."

As we continue to chat, Richard asks, "Hey, is there anything we can do to help you on your way to Santiago?"

"Well, to be honest," I reply, "we've been talking about bypassing the mountain pass into O Cebreiro—everyone keeps telling us how difficult it is."

"Quite a few people have reached out to us on Facebook, telling us to skip it," Patrick says. "One individual told us that he and some fellow pilgrims tried to take a friend in a wheelchair through the pass last year and were forced to turn back."

"So we're thinking about taking a taxi to the top instead," I say.

"Let us be your taxi to the top," Joe says enthusiastically.

This takes a moment for us to process.

"Are you guys serious?" Patrick says.

"Yeah!"

Even with all the help we've received along the way, we're still amazed at how complete strangers can be so kind and generous. After talking through some of the logistical challenges we've been told to expect at O Cebreiro, we make plans to meet Joe and Richard several weeks later at the base of the mountain, eleven miles west of the town of Villafranca del Bierzo.

After a few more minutes of conversation with our neighbors from Idaho, Patrick and I leave the house of worship and find a place where we can sit and enjoy the sun in the large square outside the cathedral. With the afternoon stretching out before us, and nowhere to go and nothing to do, we embrace our day of rest.

| | |

— PATRICK —

Our time here in Burgos is completely reshaping my thoughts about Sabbath—on what God had in mind when he gave us the concept of a day of rest.

The word *Sabbath* is believed to be derived from the Hebrew word *sabat*, which means to *stop*, to *rest*, or to *keep*. Amidst the challenge of staying connected throughout college and the constant proximity our journey has given us, this, in many ways, sums up how we approach our relationship. But taking the biblical concept of *stopping* and *resting* for a day and simply applying it to a day of the week isn't enough.

Here in Spain, Justin and I have embraced an extended Sabbath of sorts. We've slowed down and *rested* amid the pressures of life, clearing away the things that might otherwise distract us.

And we're learning how to *keep* close to us the relationships and moments that define who we are. If we didn't practice this sort of Sabbath in our friendship, if we hadn't taken this break to walk the Camino together, we'd have missed out on all of this.

Whether *resting* in my friendship with Justin or in my relationships with my wife and children, I find a greater appreciation for whoever is at my side when I take a moment to *keep* them close, to be present with them. This is something I haven't done well lately, especially with my kids. Cambria is always wanting me to read with her at bedtime, but I have only followed through a handful of times. Josh wants to wrestle with his dad, but lately, "I'm too tired tonight" is a phrase that has left my lips far too often. And little Olivia just wants to be held—a role I have left to Donna. I've been a good provider, but I've also been absent and disengaged, both physically and mentally, because of the long hours I work and the distractions that come with the stress of my job. My kids have taken a backseat to my busy schedule, early morning meetings, and late nights at the office—not to mention how dismissive and disconnected I have been because of pressures at work. I really haven't been much of a father lately. They deserve so much more than I've been giving.

But I'm becoming more aware of what they've given me, the love they have for me, and the beauty that exists in each one of them—a beauty that God longs for me to see. I'm also becoming more aware of the beauty in strangers—people like Joe and Richard and others who have helped us along the way. They are God's gift to me, but they're a gift I can't appreciate if I don't take time to *rest* with them, to *keep* them or hold them close, and let them know their value. I'm beginning to appreciate how we can practice Sabbath on any day, at any time, in any moment.

Taking the time to read a story to my son or daughter, being fully present.

Sabbath.

Taking a walk with my wife on a warm afternoon, holding her hand.

Sabbath.

Wrestling with my son, hearing his laughter as I tickle him.

Sabbath.

Lying next to my children as they drift off to sleep.

Sabbath.

Every moment we *rest* in the presence of others and appreciate the time, beauty, and joy they have to offer, we practice Sabbath. It's a mentality . . . an existence . . . a way of life.

Sitting here in this square in the middle of Spain, I'm thinking of all the damaged relationships that could be healed and the broken relationships that could be mended if we all chose to *stop* the distractions, *rest* in the presence of those we love, and *keep* them close.

In many ways, I feel this is what the Camino offers: a prolonged Sabbath allowing each person to reconnect with who they are and who God created them to be. For Justin and me, it has been a time to open our eyes to all the moments we have practiced the Sabbath lifestyle in our friendship but have not truly appreciated them for what they are.

Pushing my best friend five hundred miles through Spain in a wheelchair, meeting the helping hands and hearts of so many strangers, surrounded by God's creation.

Sabbath.

16

PURSUIT

— PATRICK —

TODAY IS FILLED WITH MIXED EMOTIONS. The rest and relaxation we've enjoyed in Burgos hardly seem enough to refill our depleted energy tanks, but both Justin and I are hungry to get back on the trail. With each passing day, the weather has grown warmer, and we strive for early starts so we can beat the heat of the warm afternoons. This morning is no exception as we rise shortly after the sun and head west.

Beyond Burgos lies a section of Spain known as the Meseta. Some refer to it as a desert, but the word literally means *plateau*. The Meseta comprises almost 40 percent of Spain's landmass, ranging in elevation from 1,300 feet to 3,300 feet. The next 150 miles of Camino trail cuts through this arid landscape, where wheat fields extend as far as the eye can see—much like Kansas. Most of the terrain is flat, and the roads are often straight for miles on end.

As we head into the first day of this long stretch, I struggle with being fully present. I am loving my time here, and there is no place I would rather be, but I feel the pressure to keep pace, to keep moving, as the end of my six-week leave draws closer with each passing day.

It has been difficult, but I have gradually shifted my focus from the destination to the journey. Still, the pressure of a career waiting across the Atlantic lingers in the recesses of my mind. I love the people I work with, but my challenging role at the hospital has been a source of monumental stress. As I work to serve the needs of the hospital, as well as those of the neurosurgeons and orthopedic surgeons I work alongside, it sometimes feels as if I'm serving two masters with diametrically opposed objectives. In spite of this distant urgency to return to the States, I am realizing these weeks on the Camino have made me happier than I've been in months. The freedom, the simplicity, and the sense of community bring a joy that is so often lacking in my daily life.

| | |

Justin and I had intended to travel well beyond the town of Hontanas today, but when we arrive, we change our minds. As we approach the small collection of buildings at the hub of the town, Joe and Richard are sitting at a table enjoying their lunch. We also see Jess from South Africa, who walked with us for a while earlier in the day before going on ahead. Her friend Claudia stayed with us and helped us on a few hills.

When we stop to rest for a few minutes, Joe and Richard introduce us to Dave from Ireland, Jessica from Australia, and Andy and his son from New York. Surrounded by the hum of voices from four different countries, we sense a feeling of oneness.

The energy here is palpable. Every person we talk to is excited to be resting and spending time with other pilgrims. Joe and Richard invite us to join their group for dinner, and we're having a hard time saying no. The need to make the day's objective has been replaced by a desire to connect with these new friends. While a few of our day's companions—including Christie—continue on, Justin and I decide to stay the night here.

There are few options for lodging in Hontanas, so we end up with bunk beds in an albergue in the center of town. After paying for our night's lodging and dropping off our bags, we head outside to enjoy the company of our fellow pilgrims.

Joe and Richard take up a collection of a few euros each from everyone, which gives them enough money to purchase food for all. While they pay a visit to the local supermercado, the rest of us retreat to a courtyard outside our albergue. In a few short hours, with the help of Jess (who, it turns out, is a chef), we are offered a table laden with pasta, a delicious meat sauce, salad, bread, and multiple bottles of Rioja wine.

As we enjoy the meal, the energy we first felt when we entered town increases tenfold.

People lean in and draw close to one another as stories are shared. There is an intentional nature here, a quality to the conversation that is beautiful to watch unfold. There's no pretense, no judgment, no hierarchy or status. We're just a group of pilgrims eagerly wanting to know more about one another, wanting to hear each other's stories and share in this beautiful moment together.

Some pilgrims talk of embarrassing moments they've experienced in coed albergues, and we all agree we've seen enough of naked strangers in the early mornings. Jess shares some of her experiences as a chef working on a yacht; Richard is wondering what to do next after graduating college; Joe is concerned about the direction of his career; and Andy is relishing the time he's spending here with his son. Others share their reasons for embarking on the Camino, and many talk of what awaits them back home and how they wish their friends and family could experience what we are experiencing now.

Hearing their stories, I'm reminded of how much I have allowed my job to keep me from having the level of connection with my family that I'm enjoying here with complete strangers. My busy schedule and my obsessive need for control at work have caused me to take on more than I should. Here in Hontanas, all the distractions have faded away, and I'm able to offer more of myself to these people than I've given to my family. For the first time, I can feel the cords that tether me to my career begin to loosen. I'm ready to give my family more of what they deserve and desire—more of *me*. But I have to choose to do so. This is what makes my friendship with Justin work, and it's one of the things that have been missing from my relationship with my wife and children.

| | |

− JUSTIN −

Staying close with Patrick over the years hasn't been easy. He and I discovered early on that we had to put forth some serious effort in order to remain connected. We made the conscious decision to make one another a priority, to pick up the phone, and to make sacrifices of time. We were willing to part with hard-earned money for plane tickets and road trips that helped to forge an enduring friendship.

Looking back on our childhood, the decisions we made to find time for each other seemed so much easier. We simply hopped on our bikes or rode our skateboards across town—but I'm not sure this is fair to say. While childhood decisions were easy and our proximity was much closer, we still had to make an active choice. We each had to decide that spending time together was worth the effort of riding our bicycles the distance between our homes. We worked in order to steal time with one another, and that time has helped us build a friendship. As adults we can become distracted from realizing how simple spending time together really is.

This kind of intentionality—this willingness to sacrifice time, to be present for one another—is especially important when tackling the challenges that tend to separate people. I think back to our college years and to the early years of our marriages.

Both Patrick and I continued to wrestle with our addictions to pornography, but for Patrick, the struggles didn't stop there. He had started smoking marijuana when we were in middle school, and this occasional habit continued into college. I still remember the phone call when he told me about the ultimatum he received from Donna: "You want to date me? Then no more weed."

Though Patrick still frequently smoked pot, he was in the throes of falling in love and desperately wanted to live up to his girlfriend's expectations. We both needed accountability and the ability to have open and honest dialogue with someone who wasn't afraid to call us out on the stupid things we convinced ourselves were okay to do.

Our obsession with pornography could have easily closed us off from one another, causing us to hide our secret, but we intentionally pursued an honest friendship. We built trust based on having each other's best interests in mind. This is what happens when we intentionally make the needs and welfare of others more important than our own.

Without experiencing this kind of vulnerable friendship, we probably would not have known how to embrace the courage Christie demonstrated when she shared her story. Being that open and honest with complete strangers takes a strength neither one of us possessed during our college years. Fortunately, we had each other to rely on, to trust, and to be vulnerable with. Any successful relationship—whether friendship or marriage—must have this level of honesty to the point of sharing anything and everything. But this can't happen if we don't pursue each other; it can't happen if we don't make time for each other. This sort of honesty can exist only if we know that, no matter what we say or do, the other person will still choose to love us and will still choose to pursue us.

| | |

— PATRICK —

I'm not sure what I would have done without the support and accountability Justin has offered me throughout our friendship. Because of the strong foundation we have, we know we can tell each other *anything*, and we can trust each other with all that we are.

This doesn't mean there haven't been times when we weren't totally honest with each other—especially about our struggles with pornography. However, more often than not, these moments are met with resistance, with loving pushback that says, "I'm sorry, man, but I don't think you're telling me the whole story. Are you sure everything's fine?"

Occasionally, one of us will call the other out and say, "You're full of crap!" Sometimes these words are hard to hear, but they're always spoken in love and always come from a heart that says, "I want what's best for you, and this isn't it."

Our pursuit of one another requires sacrifice. The effort we both choose to put into our relationship is indicative of the value we place on one another. We've both seen friendships and marriages fall apart, and every time there's been a lack of true commitment—where one or both individuals no longer puts in the effort, no longer values the relationship, no longer pursues the other person.

As adults, it can be easy to lose sight of the fact that we must pursue one another, even when it gets in the way of our own priorities. We can tell people how much we love them, how much they mean to us, but this means nothing if we don't pursue them. We have to pick up the phone, make time to be together, get in a car and make the drive, or hop on a plane and fly across the country. Like it or not, we are what we *do*, not what we say we will do. And what I've been *doing* is giving higher priority to my job than to my wife and kids. I've been a provider, but I haven't been much of a husband or father.

| | |

— JUSTIN —

The sun is now setting beyond the expanse of the Meseta, and each pilgrim is backlit by a sunset so bright they've all faded to little more than silhouettes. Patrick sits to my left, eyes closed as the sun warms his bearded face. Our hearts are filled with the love and connection shared here tonight.

Sharing a plate of food, Patrick gives me a bite of bread and helps me wash it down with a bit of wine. Bread and wine.

A group of new friends gathered around a table sharing bread and wine. Though this meal is by no means a last supper, what it represents is powerful. A community of individuals has come together around a meal, sharing the very things that will provide the energy and sustenance needed to continue moving forward.

In the Bible, the Last Supper was many things—a farewell to Jesus, the outing of a traitor in their midst, the exposition of Peter's coming denial of the Messiah. But something else happened around that table, something powerful. Jesus sought out each of these men; he pursued them and chose to break bread with them. Jesus invited them to live a different kind of life, a life of communion with him. The God of love and compassion, in whom Patrick and I choose to believe, lived his life with these men and invited them to break bread with him, to drink with him, to rest in his presence.

God's two greatest commandments are to love him and to love others.[2] But what does this kind of love look like? The only people we feel loved by are those who pursue us. They pursue conversation with us, spend time with us, hold us when we are broken, and help us get up when we fall. Their pursuit of us is what shows us we're loved. Our parents, our siblings, our wives, our kids, our friends, Ted, Christie, Joe, Richard, Claudia, John, Lynda, Bernie, Ray, and so many others—they have all pursued us in different ways. And though we are flawed and sometimes fail, we do our best to do the same.

When Patrick and I make the conscious decision to pursue one another, to actively give love and compassion to each other, we find sustenance around a very different table. We are the vessels through which the world can know God's love. In this kind of love, we find the ability to be honest about our fears and the freedom to share our failings. We find a different kind of bread to relieve a seemingly insatiable hunger, and a different kind of wine to satisfy a seemingly unquenchable thirst. Just as our bodies hunger for food and drink, our hearts long for love, our souls long to be pursued.

17

COUNTDOWN

— PATRICK —

THE LATE-NIGHT FESTIVITIES IN Hontanas mean morning seems to come earlier than usual. I wake first and dress, prep our water bottles, and pack my sleeping bag. I then wake Justin and get him ready for the day while listening to another spontaneous ditty about putting on his shoes. Then I lift him from the lower bunk and set him in his wheelchair.

Even though we are early to rise, many of our fellow pilgrims are miles down the trail before we leave the albergue. However, when we reach the road leading to the Camino trail, we find John and Claudia waiting for us. Both are planning to walk with us today. Grateful for the help and company, we head west.

Tightly packed dirt and rock make for an even path for the first part of the day. While pushing the 250 pounds of this fully loaded wheelchair is always difficult, it is remarkable how much of a difference a smooth trail makes.

With six miles of "easier" trail behind us, we pass the town of Castrojeriz. To the north of us sit the ruins of Castillo de Castrojeriz, an ancient castle atop a hill overlooking the town below. The sun is now high in the sea of blue above us, bathing our shoulders and backs in warmth. As we stop for a drink of water, Justin and I take stock of the path ahead. Directly in front of Justin's chair, the trail leads west, but in the distance it turns sharply to the left, where it traverses up to a 350-foot plateau before disappearing over the edge. As we get closer, we can see the trail turns into loose rock and gravel, a very different terrain than we have enjoyed for the first half of the day.

Claudia and John recognize the challenge and offer to pull while I push. I unclip the red nylon harness from my backpack, uncoil it, and hand it to Claudia, who clips the two carabiners at the ends of the harness to Justin's chair. Our two friends raise the harness over their heads, allowing it to rest across the front of their shoulders, and lean into the strap until it becomes taut. Taking steps in unison, they begin to pull while I push.

This section of the trail is tremendously difficult, and progress is slow as we inch our way up the hill. Soon two young Swiss women offer help and step in on either side of me. With three of us at the back and two out front, our pace briefly quickens, but the sheer force of gravity, as well as the heat of the day, has us all gasping within the next twenty feet.

This work is punishing for everyone. My calves are beginning to burn so intensely that they feel like they are going to explode, and my forearms tremble with each surge we make. John begins to fade and a passing pilgrim named Matt steps in beside Claudia. As we continue to climb, the weight pushing back on me increases as the grade steepens. My fingers are tingling with numbness from the pressure of the handlebars across my palms and the base of my thumbs, but slowly, painstakingly, we make it to the top, with Claudia pulling the entire way.

In spite of the pain and fatigue of exertion, a wave of gratitude washes over me. I find myself thanking God for each of these fellow pushers and pullers. Each one has a story, and each one is sacrificing something to be here with us. Some much more than others.

| | |

— JUSTIN —

When Claudia started walking with us yesterday, I asked her my usual question: *Tell me about yourself.* Like Christie, she quickly opened up. With a firm grip at the back of my wheelchair, she began telling her story.

She told us about how she had joined her friend Jess on the Camino at the very last minute, and how her decision to undertake the five-hundred-mile journey was grounded in making sense out of a grief and darkness that had all but consumed her over the past six months.

As we walked, Claudia talked about the most recent New Year's Eve, when she had gathered with her family in South Africa, as they always did.

"We celebrated life, enjoyed amazing food, and drank splendid wine," she said with a smile. "It was simply wonderful being together."

But when she began to describe an annual tradition of taking a family photo as the year came to a close, her voice changed. Any sense of joy at a happy memory was replaced by a stony coldness.

She described how they set up a camera with a timer to capture the photo at exactly midnight. Surrounded by her loved ones, Claudia stood smiling as the timer counted down the last ten seconds of the year. With each passing second, everyone shouted, "Ten . . . nine . . . eight . . ."

As the countdown reached zero, the camera captured the moment as masked gunmen burst into the house. In the seconds that followed, Claudia, her sister, and her mother watched as one of the intruders fired a shotgun blast at her father, striking him in the lower abdomen.

I sit in stunned silence as the reality washes over me: On New Year's Day 2014, Claudia and her family held her father as they watched the life leave his eyes.

Patrick and I have both lost loved ones, but I can't imagine watching someone I love die in such a cruel and violent way. Loss is difficult to deal with, no matter the circumstances. The effects ripple through the lives of everyone it touches. But what can we say to this?

| | |

— PATRICK —

Claudia's story fills my mind with thoughts of death and grieving. I can't begin to understand the pain she's facing.

As much as it hurts to lose a grandparent, it's expected. With each passing year, the odds of saying good-bye to the elders in our lives increase. I lost my Grandpa Gray when I was nine, and Justin said good-bye to his maternal grandmother a few years later. Over time, our remaining grandparents began to fade, and eventually they all passed. When someone dies young, though, a different dynamic is at play.

In 1988, one of my older brother's friends was killed in a motorcycle accident at the age of eighteen. Jeff had met Tony at a church camp a few summers earlier, and Tony used to come to our house to hang out or to pick up my brother for a night out. Whatever the circumstances, though, he always hunted me down, tousled my hair, and asked how I was doing. When you're thirteen and your older brother's friend seeks you out, it's a big deal. Tony was kind, full of joy, and full of life. And in the blink of an eye, he was gone.

I still remember my brother's response. It was more intense, more visceral, than when our grandpa died. I don't think it was worse, necessarily, but the pain presented differently. It seemed more emotional, more visible.

As a sophomore in high school, I went out for the track team while Justin played tennis. I wasn't fast and really had no business running track, but there was an upperclassman, Bruce, who took me under his wing and helped me train. I wouldn't say we were friends outside of my one year in track, but I appreciated his interest and the time he took to help me. The following year, he put a loaded gun in his mouth and pulled the trigger. I still remember sitting at our dining room table doing math homework when my dad walked in and gave me the news. Filled with anger and tears, I stabbed my pencil through the pages of my math book over and over.

I wasn't terribly close to either one of those young men, but I have clear memories associated with their deaths. When I close my eyes, I can still see my older brother coming down the hall toward our bedroom to give me the news about Tony. I can still hear his voice. If my memories of these deaths are so clear, I can't begin to imagine what Claudia sees when she closes her eyes.

| | |

— JUSTIN —

It has been several days since we successfully made the climb near Castrojeriz. Finishing a rest in a small room with two twin beds, Patrick and I are about to head out into the streets of the village to find something to eat. As Patrick readies himself to transfer me from the edge of the bed to my wheelchair, he looks at me and says, "It was pretty incredible the way everyone came together to get us up that hill the other day."

"I know," I say quietly while shaking my head in wonder.

"A little extra strength to help us continue on."

As Patrick says this, my phone dings, indicating a new e-mail. Assuming it's from our wives, Patrick places the phone in my lap and positions my hands so I can manipulate the touch screen.

"It's from Claudia," I say as I check my in-box. Right after the day we climbed the hill near Castrojeriz, she had gone on her way ahead of us, and we haven't seen much of her since.

"Read it," Patrick says. Somehow we both sense this is something that can't wait.

"She says she wants to thank us," I begin, "and the only way she can do this is by sharing an entry from her journal."

"Keep going," Patrick says.

"Okay, so these are her words . . ."

> *"Ready?" asks Patrick.*
> *"Yes, ready," we all reply as we flex our muscles and prepare ourselves for the exertion and exhaustion that lies ahead of us.*
> *I'm strapped into a harness at the front next*

to John, who is a sixty-year-old recycling
specialist/US Naval officer and regular at
the Burning Man festival in Nevada.

"We look like a pair of oxen," I say with a smile
to him as he wheezes and splutters next to me,
beads of sweat sliding off his chin and onto the
steep gravel path below us. While John and I do
the pulling up in the front, Patrick is pushing with
a firm grip on the steel bar at the back. He has
calves the size of spanspeks [cantaloupes] after
doing this for almost two weeks. He is flanked
by two Swiss girls we met halfway up this hill.
They started their Camino in Burgos, so they've
only been walking for two days, and their fresh,
unstable blisters are screaming at them with
every step they take. Despite the shooting pain,
they continue to push onward and upward with
the rest of us. We're only halfway up this hill and
all five of us know that giving up is not an option.

"You guys are awesome," says Justin as he
sits, strapped tightly into his wheelchair while
we slowly heave him up the hill.

As I read, I glance up at Patrick, and I can see that he is reliving that day as he listens.

Claudia's journal entry continues as she explains who Patrick and I are, why we're on the Camino, and a little about our first encounter with her:

When Justin told me about his condition, I said,
"I'm sorry to hear about that."

"There's absolutely nothing to be sorry
about!" he responded.

Back on the steep hill, we are finally within twenty metres of the top.

"The final push," gasps Patrick, while Justin sings a slightly out-of-tune rendition of "That's What Friends Are For." John, the oldest in our group by a good few decades, has tapped out, and we have replaced him with a passing pilgrim called Matt, who is now in the harness next to me, ready to pull like an ox. Patrick's sweat is cascading down his face, and the two Swiss girls next to him look like they are equal parts exhausted and excited. We've been fighting our way up this hill for almost an hour and a half.

"Ready?" asks Patrick

"Yes, ready," we all reply.

And we're off. Inching our way up. A choir of heavy breathing. As we get closer to the top, Justin begins a countdown: "Ten . . . nine . . . eight . . ."

No, I think to myself, this can't be happening. The last time I did a countdown, it was followed by unimaginable cruelty.

When it hits me what that day was like for Claudia, I have to stop to catch my breath and fight back the tears. As I begin to read again, my voice cracks.

"Seven . . . six . . . five . . ."

Maybe I should ask them to stop.

"Four . . ."

My calves are aching.

"Three . . ."

I'd be happy if I never have to endure another countdown for the rest of my life.

The tears are flowing so hard now that I have to stop reading. When I look up at Patrick, I see that his hand is over his mouth and tears are streaming down his face as well. *What did this woman give, what did she endure, just so she could help us up that hill?*

My eyes return to her journal entry:

> *"Two . . ."*
>
> *I don't know if I can do this. But I'll do it for Justin.*
>
> *"One . . ."*
>
> *We get to the top and we're hugging each other, doing a victory dance, celebrating, and kissing each other on the cheeks. And I'm crying because I didn't believe that a countdown from ten could ever be happy again.*
>
> *At the end of the day, we sip our ice-cold drinks in a small Spanish town. The sun hangs low in the sky, making me realize there must be at least a million different shades of gold and that all of them are visible during a Meseta sunset. Justin looks at me and says, "Thanks for getting me up that hill today."*
>
> *I look back at him and say, "No, Justin; it was you who got me up that hill."*

| | |

— PATRICK —

As terrible as death is, as painful as it was to watch someone she loved stolen from her, Claudia taught Justin and me a powerful lesson with her kindness, her love, and her willingness to share her story. Before that hill, she was plagued with grief and confusion, and hope was distant, if it was there at all. While Justin and I were bathed in the kindness and love that Claudia and others showed us that day, she was reliving the horror of the most terrible experience of her entire life. But because of her kindness and her willingness to help others in need, Claudia was offered a glimpse of hope, and some of the darkness associated with the violent loss of her father seemed to loosen its hold. Though we were present and clearly part of the moment that brought her some healing, we had little, if anything, to do with it. Claudia's willingness to show love and compassion to strangers, to offer help even when it cost her physically, and to push through, even when the emotional and psychological pain was crippling, gave her hope.

Claudia showed us how love and kindness have the power to lift up others. Loving and serving others is the only way we can push through the darkness that life will undoubtedly give us. Acts of unconditional love shine a light into the lives of both the giver and the receiver. A light no darkness can hide from.

18

HOW DID WE GET SO LUCKY?

− JUSTIN −

ON JUNE 19, we arrive in Carrión de los Condes, the halfway point on our journey to Santiago de Compostela. The camera crew is already in town—minus Terry, who has gone ahead to size up the trail—and they're staying in an old monastery that rents out rooms. Patrick and I decide to join them there.

Mike, Jasper, and Robin arc exhausted after two and a half weeks on the Camino and could use a nice meal, so to celebrate our progress and thank them for their dedication and hard work, we invite them to join us for dinner at a restaurant adjacent to the monastery. While these men are here to film our journey, we have drawn close to them and have developed a sort of familial bond. As we sit around the table enjoying each other's company, I'm reminded of what is waiting for me at home. Skype calls to my family have kept us connected to some degree, but I miss my kids. I miss my wife.

Sharing dinner with Kirstin and the kids is something I haven't done in weeks. On a night like tonight, we would likely head out to the park after eating and enjoy the warm summer air. My boys would beat us there on their scooters, and Lauren would either sit in my lap as I roll down the sidewalk in my power wheelchair or ride her bike beside me. At the park, Kirstin and I would sit and listen to the kids play, and just talk. All of this seems a world away.

The next morning, we take time for some interviews with the film crew in one of the many beautiful courtyards within the walls of the monastery. These up-close-and-personal conversations are important for the documentary we're filming, but they also make for a late start to the day's journey. As soon as we finish, we grab lunch in Carrión de los Condes and hit the trail.

The sky above us seems endless. With few buildings or hills to break up the skyline, the sea of blue appears to spill over the edge of the horizon. With only an occasional incline to break up the monotony of the flat, straight path, Patrick and I find ourselves completely alone in the vast expanse of the Meseta.

Normally we would cross paths with other pilgrims, but leaving town late means we are in between the daily waves of pilgrims walking from town to town. Rolling hills of wheat fields stretch to our right and left with no end in sight. Fortunately, the trail is easy going . . . at least physically.

With the ease of the trail and the lack of other pilgrims, we have taken to listening to music while we soak in the unvarying landscape. Patrick has found a cadence to his gait that keeps us moving, and each step and turn of the wheels has a rhythm that seems to match the notes of the music duo Mackintosh Braun sounding in my ears. There's a meditative element to their music, and though I hear the lyrics of each song, they don't distract me from my thoughts. My mind is still with my family, and I know Patrick is thinking about his.

Earlier in the day, he and I were discussing our wives.

"Can you believe Donna and Kirstin are letting us chase a dream halfway across the world?" I asked.

"It is pretty crazy," Patrick said. "I can't imagine life without them, but sometimes I'm surprised they love us in spite of who we are . . . at least, that's how I feel about Donna."

"I know what you mean. Kirstin has been there for me every step of the way—every appointment, every poor decision, every change in my career as a designer, every decrease in strength, and every moment of weakness. Sometimes it amazes me she's still here."

Patrick considered my words before replying. "It's pretty remarkable to have a woman love me in spite of many of the decisions I've made—and continue to make. Drugs, pornography, career changes, and lately, a job I'm so focused on that my family takes a backseat. And now here I am spending six weeks in Spain—with her full support."

Patrick continued as he pushed me down the trail, "Right now I'm not so sure I deserve what I have, but I feel blessed to have someone put so much faith in me. I just hope it's not misplaced."

Looking at the unchanging wheat fields stretching for miles all around us, I say to myself, *I know we don't deserve them. How did we get so lucky?*

| | |

— PATRICK —

The down tempo and ambient sounds of Emancipator in my earbuds match each step I take. Anytime I let my mind wander, it follows the trail back to my wife and family at home.

What are they doing right now? Are my kids crawling out of bed, going downstairs to wake Donna? Are they cuddled on the couch watching cartoons or reading books? If I were home, would I be there with them, or would I have long since left for work?

What are the fondest memories I have of my family?

I miss the laughter of my children as I wrestle with them in the living room or chase them through the house. I miss pushing them in the swings at the park across the street, or building with Legos on the floor of their bedrooms.

I miss lying next to my wife, listening to her breathing slowly as she drifts to sleep.

And it seems like a lifetime ago that Donna and I flew to southern China to meet our youngest daughter, Olivia, but I remember the joy of introducing Joshua and Cambria to their new little sister.

There are so many stories over so many years, but my recent history with my family is nothing to be proud of.

| | |

— JUSTIN —

The trail just keeps going. We can see the steeple of a small church in the distance, but after an hour it doesn't seem to be getting any closer, even though Patrick has pushed me more than three miles.

The longer we're out here, the more I miss my wife. I miss her face. I miss her voice. I miss her smile. I miss her touch. This is the longest we've ever been apart, and right now I just want her to be here.

Now that I'm away from her, I'm beginning to realize the many little things she does for me. Every morning she makes my coffee, and every afternoon we find time to sit and enjoy each other's company. I miss the conversations and the laughter. I miss her stubborn streak, which rivals my own. Through all this time with Patrick and all this time away from home, I'm learning to appreciate my wife so much more. I am grateful for a woman who loves me completely and who takes care of me and our children. In her absence, I'm beginning to appreciate the unconditional love God has for me. The love he shows me through the eyes, words, and hands of my wife.

— PATRICK —

The constant landscape of unending wheat fields, combined with a steady pace and minimal changes in elevation, makes for an interesting dynamic. Many people told us how the Meseta is mentally challenging and forces you inward, but up to this point we haven't experienced this. Now, though, the unchanging nature of our surroundings offers no distractions from my thoughts. I find myself shaking my head in an effort to brush aside what begins to fill my mind. But these thoughts, these memories, won't budge. The longer I am alone in my mind, the more they appear and the more I don't like what I see.

The humming rhythm of Justin's wheels pulls me into an almost trancelike state, and I gradually begin to see images. Random moments play on a million tiny television screens behind my eyes—frustration with my kids, dismissive words, instances of being quick to anger, times when I have failed my wife with my words, my actions, and my selfishness. Soon I can see every time I've let down my wife, every time I've disappointed my children.

My wife calls to ask when I'll be home; I tell her, "Soon," but don't make it home for several hours.

My kids ask to go to the park; I tell them, "As soon as I am done with . . ." But we never make it.

My daughter snuggles up next to me while I'm answering e-mails on my phone. I can't focus with her jostling my arm, so I get up to minimize the distraction. She looks at me, but I avoid eye contact.

I have my phone at the table and answer calls from physicians late into the evening. "That phone is keeping you from your family!" my wife says to me. "This phone is helping put food on the table!" I reply in anger.

Normal brother-and-sister squabbles among my kids are met with angst and a raised voice instead of with love and a desire to understand how they're feeling.

Expectant eyes look to me for hugs or even just a smile, but I walk by, pretending not to see them. I pretend I don't see the hurt because I don't have the time or patience to deal with it.

"I miss you, Daddy!" I hear over and over, but I don't make any change.

Now, every moment I wish I could take back is staring me in the face as if to say, *This is who you are! What are you going to do about it?* Taking all of this in at once, absorbing all my failings as a father and as a husband, brings me to silent tears as I push Justin down the path ahead of us.

I don't know what to make of this, but I don't like what I see and I don't like who I've been in each of these moments. I've never been abusive or cruel, but I've been so neglectful and dismissive. I haven't led in love, and I have given my children and my wife reasons to question how much I value them, reasons to doubt how much I love them. I haven't spent time in Sabbath with them. I haven't pursued them.

When we arrive in the next town, I am desperate to speak to my family. We find a coffee shop with wi-fi and I place a Skype call, hoping they'll all be awake. When Donna answers, surrounded by our kids, the words pour from my aching heart.

"Cambria, Joshua, and Olivia, I love you all so much," I say as my voice cracks. I have told them I love them a million times, but never quite like this.

Cambria smiles and asks, "Why are you crying?"

"Because I haven't shown you how much I love you. I am so sorry for all the times I have let you down."

Joshua and Olivia tell me they love me and miss me, but Cambria, my oldest, says to me, "I forgive you, Daddy, and I love you, too."

After some time with my kids, I ask them for a few moments to speak to their mother alone. As Donna sits in the quiet of our office with the door closed, halfway across the world, I tell her, "I am sorry for every time I have broken your heart, and I know there have been many." At this point, I am crying almost uncontrollably.

Donna just smiles as she takes a moment to respond. Her voice is tender but deliberate as she says, "If you never broke my heart, how would I learn to love you more?"

These words strike me in a way I'm not expecting. The confession of my failings has given my wife an opportunity to love me or hate me for what I have done, for who I have been. Her choice to forgive me, to look past my faults and continue to take my hand, strips my failures of any power in my life. This never could have happened if I didn't trust her with all of me.

As weird as it may seem, being entirely accountable offers others an opportunity to show the depth of their love. It gives them the opportunity to demonstrate how there are no conditions to their love.

Though Donna said it only once, I keep replaying her words in my head.

If you never broke my heart, how would I learn to love you more?

19

WE'RE NOT ALONE IN HERE

— JUSTIN —

WHILE THE MESETA CONTINUES to challenge us mentally and emotionally, the past few days have taken a physical toll on Patrick. The constant day in, day out of pushing the chair has affected his legs, and he now has significant pain and cramping in his calves that no amount of stretching seems to alleviate. We had planned to take a rest day here in the city of León, but Patrick's discomfort now has us questioning whether we should take two days to allow him more time to recuperate. With nineteen days and 280 miles behind us, he has more than earned an extra day of rest.

We opt for beds in a quaint hotel with rooms large enough to accommodate my wheelchair. Our room overlooks a large city square that is surprisingly empty for a Sunday afternoon. Adjacent to the hotel is the albergue where many pilgrims are staying, including Christie. Having decided to stay two nights in León, we let Christie know, but we haven't seen Lynda or John, who have opted for another albergue. Once settled, we set out to explore the city. After dinner, both full and satisfied, we return to our room for showers and a good night's sleep.

Unfamiliar voices invade my dreams, and as they get louder and louder, I wake. Eyes open in the dark room, I realize the voices aren't just in my head. Apparently Patrick can hear them, too, because he's standing at the window looking down at the square below.

"There must be a couple hundred people down there," he says when he sees I'm awake.

"What time is it?"

"Two in the morning"

"What are they doing?"

"Singing. Dancing. Having a good ol' time!"

Like Burgos, León is a large city, but it has a different feel. The streets are quieter during the day, and the nightlife is definitely more vibrant and celebratory—at least tonight. We do our best to block out the noise, but there is so much laughter drifting up to our window, we find it difficult not to smile as we drift to sleep. Somehow, in spite of the sounds and voices, we get some much-needed rest and wake to the sun shining through our window. As morning draws closer to noon, we finally get dressed for the day, and Patrick stuffs our filthy, sweat-stained clothes into his backpack. We desperately need to do laundry.

Once again, the city is quiet as we navigate our way to the nearest Laundromat. We wash our clothes, and while we wait for them to dry, the streets gradually get busier.

Christie has also decided to spend the day in León, and she joins us now in our exploration of the city. Well into the afternoon, we wander through town and chat with many of the locals. My wheelchair is a bit of an anomaly, and people are curious about why I'm here. When Patrick and I explain our journey and mention that we've come all the way from St. Jean Pied de Port, many people simply refuse to believe us. That a man in a wheelchair could have traveled this far is beyond their comprehension.

Outside a coffee shop, a man asks us in broken English if we are doing the Camino.

"Yes, we are!"

"Where did you start?" he asks.

"St. Jean," Patrick replies as he lifts a cup of coffee to my lips.

"How was the bike route on your chair?"

"We didn't take the bike route. We went over the top, on the Napoleon Route."

The gentleman laughs and says, "No, you didn't."

We talk with him for a few more minutes before we leave the café, but he remains unconvinced.

The afternoon turns to evening, and with the setting sun comes hunger. We pick up some food to take back to the room, and when we reach the courtyard outside our hotel, we have to navigate our way through an even bigger crowd than last night. We wonder what's going on, but we're more tired than curious, so we turn in.

I haven't had my eyes closed nearly long enough before screaming and yelling erupts from just below our window. Two nights in a row, we've been awakened at 2:00 a.m. Tonight, however, the celebration is ten times louder, and I can see the dancing flicker of flames reflected on the window from a bonfire below. Even though I'm exhausted, the laughter rising up to our window makes me smile, just like last night. Lying here in the middle of the night, with Patrick at the window, I am reminded of a very different set of circumstances when he and I were pulled from sleep in the wee hours of the morning.

| | |

Growing up, my family had a 1950s cabin in Donnelly, Idaho, about 120 miles northeast of Ontario, near McCall. Patrick frequently accompanied my family on weekend excursions, and he and I would explore the woods, shoot BB guns, and walk down to the lake to fish (though I don't think we ever caught anything).

When I proposed to Kirstin, she and I were staying at the cabin with my family. I still remember asking Patrick to come up to Donnelly without Kirstin knowing. He took a camera and hid in the bushes across a narrow stretch of a nearby lake. When I popped the question, he captured the moment on film.

After we'd been married for several years, Kirstin and I had officially established the habit of taking a trip with Patrick and Donna every year. One particular year, when money was tighter than usual, we extended the length of our visit to Ontario to allow us to spend several days with Patrick and Donna at my family's cabin. They had recently moved to a town near Boise, so the trip to Donnelly was a short drive for all of us.

The small red-and-white A-frame was nothing to speak of, but we had so many memories associated with the tiny living space. Downstairs boasted a family room with a wood stove, a small dining area, a kitchen, and one bathroom. Up a narrow set of stairs were two bedrooms connected by a small hallway. As boys, Patrick and I had always slept in tents on the property, but that night—the first time the four of us had ever stayed at the cabin together as couples—we were looking forward to the comfort of the queen-size beds.

An evening of barbecued burgers, snacks, and board games kept us up late, laughing. Midnight came sooner than we expected, and we finally decided to turn in. By this point in my life, stairs had become difficult for me, but with the support from my leg braces, I was still able to make the ascent. At the top of the stairs, Kirstin and I turned right and headed into the back bedroom while Patrick and Donna turned left.

As we crawled into bed, the pale moonlight shining through the Juliet balcony in Patrick and Donna's room offered a faint light into ours.

I had been asleep for maybe an hour when I felt something brush my face, followed by a rustling sound somewhere in the room. Confused, I peered through the darkness, hoping to figure out what was happening. When I heard the rustling again, I nudged Kirstin.

"Honey, I think there's something in here."

Annoyed and not fully awake, she said, "No, there's not. Go back to sleep."

I closed my eyes again, but not a minute later I felt the same sensation on my face. Brushing at it wildly while shaking my head, I felt the wings of something flap as it flew away.

"Kirstin! Turn on the light! I think there's a bird in here!"

Irritated at me for waking her again, she reluctantly reached for the bedside lamp. As soon as the light came on, I saw a black winged shadow dart across our room and out into the hallway leading to Patrick and Donna's side of the cabin.

"Crap! It's a *bat*!"

| | |

— PATRICK —

Sometime after we had all gone to bed that night, I awoke to the sound of Justin and Kirstin whispering loudly in their bedroom, but nothing was clear enough to register until the soft light from the bedside lamp in their room dully illuminated ours. With eyes now open, I saw a black shadow dart across our room as Justin yelled, "Crap! It's a *bat*!"

Fully awake now, I scrambled out of bed to grab my boxers. As I pulled them on, Justin came into the room, using the walls to steady himself as he walked.

"Pat! There's a bat in here! It just flew into your room!"

"I know. I think it's on the floor on Donna's side of the bed."

"What!" Donna yelled as she pulled the covers over her face to shield herself from our unwanted guest. Only her long brown ponytail stuck out from under the covers. As I crept around the end of the bed to her side, I could see the bat lying on the floor with its wings spread flat against the carpet.

"What do we do?" I asked Justin.

"Use your T-shirt," he suggested, pointing to my shirt on the floor. "See if you can throw it on him and scoop him up, then throw him out the window."

As I leaned down to retrieve my shirt, Justin grabbed a decorative pillow at the end of the bed to use as a shield—or a weapon.

"If that thing flies up," he said, "I'm gonna whack it with this pillow!"

Somehow, we both felt equipped for the job.

I squatted a few feet away from the furry creature so I had some distance in case it flew at me. Slowly, so as not to frighten the bat, I leaned as far forward as possible and tossed my shirt onto our unwelcome visitor.

Nothing happened. The bat lay motionless.

Feeling a little braver, I started to scoop up the T-shirt while gathering it around the bat's body, but a series of loud squeaks erupted from beneath my hands.

"IT MAKES NOISE?!?" Kirstin yelled from the other room. "IT MAKES NOISE?!?"

Donna just let out a loud, "EEEW!" as she kicked her legs under the covers in disgust.

Determined to get rid of this thing as quickly as possible and return to bed, I tried to pick up the bundle of T-shirt and winged intruder, but somehow he worked his way free and flew directly at me—waist high. What happened next, I never could have imagined.

| | |

– JUSTIN –

The pillow I picked up was filled with some kind of stuffing that gave it some weight. Setting a wide stance to keep my balance, I stood at the ready as Patrick bent down to gather up the bat. When we heard the squeaks, I saw Patrick's eyes grow wide with fear as he shouted, "OH NO!" and began dancing out of the way of the black missile flying toward him. As Patrick tried to avoid the oncoming threat, his boxers shifted and he was left completely . . . unprotected.

At the very last second, the bat veered away from Patrick and flew directly at me. Without hesitation, I took a swing that would have made Babe Ruth proud. As the pillow connected with it, the bat pinwheeled through the air and landed on the front of Patrick's boxers.

As the unwanted visitor latched onto the fabric of Patrick's underwear and began flapping its wings against his skin, Patrick shouted, "IT'S ON MY JUNK! IT'S ON MY JUNK!"

The sensation of furry wings in a place they should never be had caused Patrick to completely lose his mind.

By now, both Donna and Kirstin were laughing hysterically from the safety of their respective hiding places, and I stood, pillow in hand, ready to swing again at a moment's notice.

Filled with absolute terror, Patrick raised a closed left fist and swung toward the winged creature, hoping to dislodge it from his boxers. But in his panic, he was a little off target. Instead of striking the bat with a force meant to stun—if not kill—the animal, Patrick delivered the deathblow directly to his own manhood.

I laughed so hard I could barely stand up. Lying at my feet was a completely dazed bat, and a few feet away Patrick was writhing on the floor, groaning and cupping himself in an attempt to ease the self-inflicted pain.

After several minutes, he recovered, threw his shirt over the still-bewildered bat, and launched the entire wad of cotton fabric and fuzzy wings out the balcony window.

Problem solved, Patrick and I just looked at each other in disbelief. Not sure what to do next, I simply shrugged and said, "Well, good night."

We all had a hard time getting back to sleep as we kept breaking out in spontaneous laughter.

| | |

— PATRICK —

It's 5:00 a.m., and the party in the square has finally ended. Justin and I embrace the quiet and choose to sleep in a little later than usual. But soon the sun shining through our window is too bright, so we get up, get ready, and head out for breakfast. Our curiosity gets the best of us, and we ask around about the previous night, which was so much louder than the night before. It turns out that today, June 24, marks the Feast of St. John the Baptist. Last night's ruckus was the annual celebration of St. John's Eve, the most festive of several nights leading up to the day honoring the birth of John the Baptist.

Being awakened by a party celebrating the birth of a saint and being dragged from sleep by a wayward bat are hardly comparable stories, but neither one would have happened if not for the intentional nature of our friendship. So many memories have been made—and are being made here on the Camino—because of our commitment to one another.

We know people who choose isolation over relationship but then are jealous of the stories and memories others share about their spouses, siblings, parents, and friends. There is a longing for connection, yet something keeps them from fully engaging in their relationships. This desire for human connection is what has many pilgrims on the Camino. But intentional, purposeful commitment can be difficult.

Many of us commit to spending time with friends and family on holidays like Christmas (or the celebration of St. John last night). After all, holidays require our attention only a few times a year. But the quality of the memories made is often determined by the depth of our relationships. This depth comes only by sacrificing time and effort, and by fully engaging in relational living. A depth that is the result of bearing witness to one another's lives.

I can't help but think that much of the laughter we heard last night was the product of friends and family intentionally and purposefully spending time together. How many stories, filled with joy and laughter, occurred last night because of this intentional nature? How many more would occur if each day were lived with this same commitment to one another?

20

PRIDE AND JOY

— PATRICK —

DESPITE THE LOUD NIGHTS IN León celebrating the life of John the Baptist, we found the rest we needed, and today is our second day back on the trail. Our extra rest day means John and Lynda are farther down the trail, but Christie is still walking with us, and we enjoy her company and appreciate her help.

As we leave Villavante and head toward Astorga, we are anxious to leave this last leg of the Meseta behind us. My calves are feeling great, but I'm starting to get nervous about work again. My anxiety has shifted from feeling the pressure of needing to finish the Camino in time to get back to my obligations within our set timeline, to wondering whether I want to go back to my job at all. My position offers a remarkable amount of security, but it comes at a cost. The money is good and the benefits are great, but I haven't been fully present for my wife and kids in months. They have suffered because of the very job I think I need in order to care for them. In the process of providing financial stability, I have failed to provide love, time, and affection. And at what cost? There is no price I can place on these things.

Seeing how Justin has lived out his faith over the past decade—stepping out on his own as a freelance graphic designer despite the uncertainty of his illness—I'm beginning to wonder whether my commitment to doing what is best for my family financially has actually been an excuse for living in safety and becoming complacent. Every job I've ever had has been one I've been asked to apply for. I have never stepped out in faith. The safety I have known because of this has kept me from discovering what I am capable of; it has kept me from experiencing what God is capable of. My kids deserve more than this.

While my thoughts about returning to work are conflicting, Justin and I have revisited our four-year-old dream of finding a way to work together. But there aren't many businesses that combine the skills of a graphic designer and a nurse, at least not any that come to mind. The trail ahead is filled with short but steep ascents and descents, and the strain of this new series of challenges distracts me from my thoughts about work and my kids.

The number of hills increases as we draw closer to Astorga, and I'm grateful that Christie has chosen to walk with us today. Her pulling out front has made the last half of the day possible. But as we enter town and find ourselves on pavement, we have one more extremely sharp incline to navigate.

As Christie straps in and begins to pull with everything she has, I tell her, "Thank you for all your help over the past week."

"Thanks for letting me walk with you," she replies.

Our breathing soon becomes labored as we work our way slowly up the steep street. As we reach the halfway point, our combined strength is no longer enough. We are now at a complete standstill, with no one around to shout to for help. I'm pressing my entire body into the back of the chair while Christie leans into the nylon strap across her shoulders. Together we hold our position and consider what to do next.

My legs are starting to shake, and I'm completely drenched in sweat. I look desperately up to the apex of the hill as a black BMW comes over the crest. The car rolls slowly past us, and a young Spanish man leans out the driver's side window and yells for us to hang on. With one quick turn of the wheel, he pulls his car across both lanes of traffic, preventing anyone from approaching us from behind. With the engine still running, he jumps out of his car, steps in beside me, grabs hold of the handlebar, and helps us push Justin to the top. When the road levels out, he turns and runs back to his illegally parked car. As he climbs in, he shouts, *"¡Buen Camino!"* and drives off.

We don't have a chance to properly thank him. We don't even know his name. But somewhere there's a mother and father who should be proud of their son. I can't help but wonder, *Am I teaching my kids to respond to situations like this man did?* I honestly don't know.

While my mind is filled with thoughts of doing things differently with my kids, I'm reminded that today is the day we're scheduled to meet up with Amee Hardy (Ted's wife) and a few boys from the boarding school in Idaho where she works.

Amee is a licensed counselor who helps young men deal with behavioral problems that affect their ability to learn. Every year, a few of the boys earn a trip out of the country for their hard work and progress in school. This year they selected Spain as their destination, and tomorrow these young men will walk with us on the Camino.

After Justin, Christie, and I work our way through town to

find lodging, we head for a nearby restaurant, where we connect with Amee and coordinate plans for tomorrow.

Under a few umbrellas outside a restaurant, we sit with Amee, her fellow chaperone, Kahn, and the young men who have made the trip across the ocean and plan to walk with us in the morning.

As we eat our lunch, Justin asks, "How's Ted?"

"He's good, and it's good to have him home," Amee says, "but I think he wishes he were still here. He misses the trail. He misses you guys."

"We miss him," I interject. "We wouldn't have made it here without him."

As the conversation continues, I can see the four young men are growing restless. Anxious to keep them occupied, we finish our lunch and begin a casual walking tour of the town's streets, culminating in a visit to the Episcopal Palace of Astorga, an imposing, castle-like granite building that also houses the Los Caminos Museum. On our way back to the hotel, we get the boys some ice cream and finalize our plans for tomorrow with Amee and Kahn.

| | |

— JUSTIN —

In the morning, Patrick has us both up and ready to go by 6:30 a.m. As we leave our room, Patrick is unknowingly humming the tune to the song I just sang for him: "There's Pat, puttin' on my shirt, puttin' on my shirt." I can't help but laugh to myself.

As we make our way to the nearby restaurant where we'll meet Amee and the boys, the sun casts long shadows as it rises out of the east and begins to warm the streets. We haven't been waiting long before Christie shows up, along with Tiffanie, another pilgrim who has walked with Christie occasionally over the past week. Soon after, Amee, Kahn, and the boys arrive. With the film crew in tow, we set out for the 14.6-mile trek to Rabanal del Camino.

The road out of town is flat, and the morning is quickly warming. The boys are all eager to push me, but Patrick is at the helm for this first stretch. Navigating city streets often means my chair must be lifted up and down tall curbs, and this is something the boys aren't quite strong enough to do. But as soon as we're west of Astorga, they begin taking turns pushing me along the trail while Patrick, Christie, and Tiffanie walk with Amee and Kahn.

The rotation of pushers quickly dwindles from four to three, and after a couple of hours, only two boys are still willing to keep me moving. By the third hour, we're down to only one young man who is still pushing me, but he is having the time of his life. He stops to rest more often than I'm used to, but he's half Patrick's size, so I give him some grace. Each time we stop, he checks to make sure I'm okay—and even though sweat is pouring down his face and he looks like he's in pain, there is so much joy in his eyes. Patrick has offered several times to give him a break, but he just keeps putting one foot in front of the other.

This kid—this servant! His joy is infectious, and I can't help but be happy. More than three months have passed since this wheelchair first arrived at Patrick's house and our six young kids followed us around the park on the inaugural test drive. On our second lap, each of our children pushed me briefly, and now this young man pushes me. Kids can be filled with so much tenacity, so much joy, and so much acceptance. I am appreciating how much of a gift they are.

My role as a father has evolved as my disease has progressed.

There are many things I wish I could still do with my sons and daughter. I can no longer play catch, swing a tennis racket, or wrestle with them, but I can still try to teach them the important things in life. I'm trying to teach them to love their fellow man and to help when needed. I'm trying to teach them to respond to life's situations the way the man in the BMW did yesterday and the way the young man pushing me is doing now.

| | |

Between Patrick's family and mine, we have six amazing children, all very different and all special in so many ways. Jaden, my eldest, has been active and athletic ever since he was born in September 2003. Because I was still able to walk when he was a child, we wrestled and played games of hide-and-seek.

In April 2005, after Patrick graduated from nursing school, his eldest daughter, Cambria, came into the world. The excitement of being parents was now something Kirstin and I could share with Patrick and Donna.

Cambria has an inquisitive nature and bright mind, something she shares with Noah, my other son, who joined the Skeesuck clan in late August the same year.

With our increasing numbers, our annual getaways became more difficult to arrange, so we started going to each other's homes instead. Either we would visit the Grays in Idaho or they would come to San Diego to see us. Shortly after Noah was born, I began using a manual wheelchair full-time, but I could still get out of it, lie down on the ground, and wrestle with my boys and Cambria. Together, Patrick and I would toss the kids around, tickle them, and pin them to the ground with kisses.

In October 2008, Patrick's son, Joshua, entered the world,

followed by my daughter, Lauren, the next March. Josh came out moving to music, and Lauren loved art and princesses from the start.

In October 2009, the Grays' younger daughter, Olivia, was born halfway across the globe in southern China. It would be another seven months before she would meet her family, but Patrick and Donna were overjoyed to have finally made their family complete.

By the time Olivia came home, my ability to play with the kids was limited. I could no longer push them in the swings, play hide-and-seek, or play catch. Fatherhood was looking different with each passing year. However, the evolution of my disease and the fact that I was living life from a wheelchair didn't seem to matter to my children, nor did it matter to Patrick's. They never saw me as a man in a wheelchair; they just saw me as Dad or Uncle Justin.

Though I couldn't run through the yard in a game of tag or throw the kids over my shoulder the way Patrick could, this became something he did for me. It was difficult to give this up, but I could either choose to be angry or embrace it. I chose the latter.

For years, Patrick and I dreamed of living closer to one another so he could do many of the things with my kids that I can't. Now that we live close by in Idaho, that dream is a reality. I have come to see it as a gift that we give to each other—a gift that is shaping my children, just as it is shaping his.

| | |

— PATRICK —

On the trail, Justin and I have talked a great deal about fatherhood, about our kids. He's had to give up so many elements of being a father—playing games, wrestling, building forts, playing tag in the front yard, and climbing trees—but I've been blessed to be able to do all of these precious things, both with his children and my own.

But after our time in the Meseta, I realize I haven't relished the moments of laughter and play as much as I should have, at least not recently. Each of these moments should be a reminder of the joys in life and how beautiful time spent with our children can be. I have lost sight of the wonders that are my kids. And while these moments are important, they are not what is most important. I have been missing out on something else as well.

Whether a man can run and wrestle like I can or lives life from a power chair like Justin, as a father he can offer the most important things to his children. Every interaction with our kids is an opportunity to facilitate trust, demonstrate accountability, and show love.

Our words can give our children the freedom to explore new ideas and develop their own faith, or our words can tear down their self-esteem. How we behave in a game of basketball or while building a fort can be just as powerful a demonstration of how we should value other human beings as the words we choose when addressing our wives.

As fathers, we show our sons how a woman should be treated and what our daughters should expect from a man through what we say and do, and how we say and do it. This happens whether we are playing games, washing dishes, or working hard to pay the bills. In every situation, our words, actions, and demeanor paint a picture of who our children think they should be.

As the young boy next to me pushes Justin in spite of the pain and exhaustion, I feel a sense of pride in him. I hope his parents are able to see the beauty and tenacity that are inside this young man. The gentleman in the BMW yesterday demonstrated love and generosity in a few short minutes, and I'm grateful for having met him and for the people in his life who helped instill those values. With each step I take, I consider my own kids and what I want them to see when they look at me. Who do I want them to become and how do I want them to live their lives?

The Camino has made this much clear to me: I want my life to demonstrate love, sacrifice for others, compassion, and value placed in relationships. I want my life to be a compass for my children to use as a guide for how they should live theirs, and I am suddenly and painfully aware of how I have been failing my beautiful children.

At the end of the day, Justin and I sit at a small table outside of an albergue. I turn to him and say, "I don't want to go back to who I was."

"What do you mean?"

"Through clinging to the safety and financial security of a job that is consuming me, I have shown my children that money is more important than love, and success is more important than relationship. I have been blind to how my job is eroding the bonds I have with my kids and Donna."

"What do you think will happen if you continue down this path?" Justin asks.

"I don't know, but I don't want to find out. I have already become stale and disengaged from my family. I have made decisions based on financial comfort, and the very thing I want my children to see most in me is the one thing that is missing."

Justin stares at me unblinking. "What's missing?"

"I have placed all my faith in myself. I've placed little in those around me and virtually none in God. More than anything else, I want the faith that guides me, that pushes you along, to be the same faith that guides my children. That's what's missing!"

I lean forward and rest my head in my hands and continue.

"I have played it safe and have let my fears take too much control. As a result, I have completely limited what God can do in my life. Not because he can't, but because I won't let him."

"What aren't you letting him do?"

Raising my head, I look at my best friend. "I'm not sure yet, but I'm ready to find out."

Amazing, these children of ours. They bring us so much joy and happiness, and yet they challenge us. When we look past their eyes and into their souls, the character we see is a reflection of who we are—our life choices, our successes, our joys, our fears, and our pain. But here in the town of Rabanal del Camino, I am looking less at who my kids are and more at who I want them to be. Not focusing on the career path or the résumé, but rather the spirit they will one day possess. When I look at who I want them to be and compare it to who I am right now, a powerful light shines on the person I no longer want to be. There is more for them than what I am living. I just need to find it.

I know it's in here somewhere.

21

WHO DO YOU THINK YOU ARE?

— PATRICK —

IT'S 3:00 A.M. My word, this is *early*. Christie and Tiffanie plan to meet us outside at 3:30. We all want to get to Cruz de Ferro, the Iron Cross, before sunrise. There are no songs from Justin this morning as I quickly help him into his clothes and brush his teeth.

At 5,020 feet, Cruz de Ferro is the highest point on the Camino, and for centuries, it has served as a landmark for leaving things behind. Pilgrims traditionally bring a stone or a memento from home to leave at the foot of this cross. None of us are sure what to expect.

Outside, we assemble in the chilly morning air. Christie and Tiffanie are ready and eager to start the day's hike. Before we go, I bundle Justin into his flannel-lined chaps and fleece jacket, tucking his hands into the insulated pockets to protect them from the cold. Reaching into his pack at the back of the wheelchair, I retrieve his wool stocking cap, pulling it down over his ears as I slide it toward the back of his head to keep it from covering his eyes.

The darkness requires us to don our headlamps. After pulling

Justin's over his wool cap, I push the button on the top and then put on mine. Christie and Tiffanie flash theirs at us to let us know they are ready to begin.

As we venture out onto the ascending trail, four beams of light are all that disturb the predawn. The hill is not very steep, but the incline is steady and long. Christie straps in up front to pull while I push; Tiffanie walks alongside, awaiting her turn in the rotation. This early in the morning, our bodies are awake, but not our minds. There is little conversation for the first hour. My thoughts over the past few days—about my family, about my future—still weigh heavily on my mind.

It is now 4:30 a.m., and we're moving slower than expected. There is no way we will make it to the cross by sunrise. Trudging on, we begin to talk more while occasionally looking back to the east to see if the sun is catching up to us. Eventually we see the thin line of light that announces dawn's arrival, and we decide to stop to rest at Foncebadón and enjoy a quick café con leche. Standing outside, we find ourselves gazing at an immaculate sunrise.

Justin's breath creates small white clouds as he says, "It still amazes me how far we've come."

I just stare at the orange, pink, and yellow pressing into the dark blue, releasing a new day.

Soon, it is time to get moving again. The sunrise has beaten us to Cruz de Ferro, but daylight is waiting for us there. With a little less than a mile to go, we cover the remaining distance relatively quickly.

From a distance, we can see the iron cross, which sits atop a tall pole, but none of us appreciates the stones at the base of the towering monument until we get much closer. There must be a million of them, maybe more. I feel a heaviness I haven't figured out yet.

In 2001, Justin and I, along with our wives, visited Dachau, the Nazi concentration camp. When we stepped across the threshold that separated the grounds of the camp from the public street, we could feel a weight, an unseen force that pressed in on us from every angle. An invisible boundary marked the location of so much sorrow, pain, and death. Though the heaviness is different here, we notice a similar change as we cross another unseen boundary. As I push Justin to the base of the mound, a quiet reverence fills the air and we feel the weight increase, a force that is difficult to explain. A few other pilgrims are here, but no words are spoken.

The sheer number of stones left behind over hundreds of years makes me wonder how much grief and loss have been left here. Pictures of lost loved ones sit under a number of stones; others are nailed to the pole that supports the cross. Farewell letters and notes of forgiveness sit anchored by small rocks everywhere we look. I feel a tightness in my chest, and a lump wells in my throat. This is holy ground.

Behind us, we hear laughter as another group of pilgrims nears the cross. Turning to watch their approach, we see their countenance change as they cross the invisible line. They slow their gait, silence their voices, and lift their eyes from the stones on the ground to the cross that points skyward. Justin and I begin to talk quietly about what we might leave here. As I turn a small medallion between my thumb and forefinger, Justin asks, "Is that the prayer angel Becca gave you?"

"Yeah, it is."

"What are you going to do with it?"

| . | |

Becca's office is two doors down from mine. For the past four years, we have worked together and drawn close as friends, facing many of the same struggles in our jobs.

On my last day of work before leaving for Spain, Becca came into my office and placed a small pewter medallion in my hand. A simple outline of an angel stared back at me.

"I will be praying for your safety along the journey," she said.

"Thank you."

"Do you think you'll come back to this?"

"Yeah, what else would I do?"

"I don't know."

We've been given so much on this journey—money, resources, a bike, a wheelchair, and many hours of help—but sometimes it's the smallest of gifts that have the greatest impact.

At the base of this mound of stones, I look at Justin and am reminded of how much he has already left behind.

| | |

— JUSTIN —

Staring at Patrick, I can see he's wrestling with what he knows he needs to leave here at the foot of this cross. I know what he's feeling because I've been there myself.

The night I drove my beloved Toyota Tundra for the last time is still vivid in my memory.

I remember the dark sky peppered with the tiny lights of distant stars.

I remember the streets empty of people as I attempted to walk the short distance from my truck to my front porch.

I remember the shock and pain of my legs giving out as my cane was no longer enough to keep me upright.

I remember the sound of my knees hitting the walkway.

I remember the struggle to get back up, only to fall twice more, each fall harder than the one before.

I remember the coolness of the concrete against my face and hands as I dragged myself along the path toward the porch.

But what I remember most are the tears that flowed and the words I spoke.

For years, prayers for healing had been lifted to the heavens with no answer. An unknown diagnosis with no cure, no effective treatment, and no prognosis for how long my life would last, just the knowledge that the end is coming—these things had taken their toll.

Through my tears and confusion, I looked at the twinkling lights dotting the sky and broke the quiet of the night as I spoke to the emptiness above.

"God, I don't know why this is happening, but if you're not going to heal me, at least make this mean something! Let me be your vessel, let me be your light, because I don't know what else to do."

In that moment, I finally took hold of my unknown future. I embraced a life filled with questions and few answers. Peace consumed me like a warm bath after a cold rain. Whether it had been set in motion years earlier or was an answer to my prayer that day, I couldn't begin to understand how much this moment would mean someday.

Four years later, in January 2010, Kirstin and I were in the throes of parenthood. Lauren had been born the previous year. Our two boys—Jaden, six, and Noah, four—and our nine-month-old daughter kept us incredibly busy.

I had perfected life in my manual wheelchair. The disease had taken my legs, but I could navigate our new house, take care of the kids, and complete the many graphic design projects that paid the bills. Life wasn't just manageable; life was good.

A thousand miles to the north, Patrick and Donna lived with their five-year-old daughter, Cambria, and two-year-old son, Joshua, in Meridian, a suburb of Boise, Idaho. Their family would soon be complete. In a few short months, they were headed to China to adopt their third child, little Olivia.

We were always in constant communication with each other, so Patrick was fully aware of my life with a wheelchair. The four of us had traveled so much together; he really had no worries for me. The disease had remained at my waist or below for several years. There was no sign of progression in sight, and a successful graphic design career left little reason for concern.

| | |

It always begins with twitching. Slight spasms foreshadow much worse things to come. Late in January new spasms arrived. The dreaded sensation grew in my right upper shoulder. And as these twitches increased in frequency and intensity, weakness was soon to follow. Historically, the changes had come slowly. This time was different. A rapid decay of strength and coordination was revealing itself. What began in my right shoulder soon attacked my left shoulder, then both arms. My lower abdominal muscles and hands began to fail. Within a month and a half, I lost nearly 70 percent of my upper body's function.

My upbeat demeanor faded as the magnitude of the situation, the reality of what this all meant, began to sink in. The weight of it all resulted in darkness and depression—unwanted companions.

For the first time in my life, I was facing a hole that was black and bottomless. Empty. It was a frightening place to be, and the temptation to let myself fall into the hole seemed as powerful as gravity. At first, it pulled slowly, but with each passing day the force seemed to grow.

I began to think, *If I kill myself, I kill the burden.*

By now, several weeks had passed since I first lost so much use of my hands. The impact this was having on my wife, on my kids, was overwhelming. Kirstin now had to dress me and bathe me. She had to help me go to the bathroom. She had to cut my food for me and lift the fork to my lips.

Sitting at the edge of the abyss, I asked myself, "How can I place this on my wife? How can I put my children through this? How can I let my friends endure this?"

I thought about driving my wheelchair into oncoming traffic or off a cliff, or drowning myself in our tub. Suicide had become a very real option, a way to end the burden, to take away the darkness.

As thoughts of taking my own life filled my head each day, I revisited that night alone on my front porch, and now I was questioning whether the moment was real or I had imagined it. It seemed so long ago, but the peace I had felt was real, and though it seemed distant, all I had to do was turn from the darkness and let the peace of that moment counter the fear that welled inside me. It took a conscious decision to focus on the peace, and though it has never completely taken away the darkness, the peace shines brightly enough that only distant shadows remain.

Convinced this would one day mean something, I made the conscious decision to turn my back on the blackness and let light show me the way. Somehow, some way, something great would come from all of this.

And so a new season of adapting began. Everything had to be relearned: eating, drinking, brushing teeth, showering, going to the bathroom, and getting dressed. Every aspect of life presented a brand-new set of challenges.

My graphic design work continued, but I was definitely slowing down with limited use of my hands. Using newly acquired voice-automated software, what had once taken forty hours to finish now took sixty or more. The writing was on the wall. My design career was coming to a close.

| | |

— PATRICK —

Before Justin lost the use of his hands, I was able to support him through our friendship with little fear of his disease. But the sudden shift in his condition profoundly affected every part of me—darkening my mind, heart, and soul. On a phone call in February 2010, when Justin told me about the sudden and drastic loss of strength and function in so many of his muscles, I realized this was the first time he was frightened about his future.

When I saw that he could no longer hold a cup to drink or lift a bite of food to his lips, I began to pray for healing, for some sort of divine intervention on my friend's behalf. I prayed more fervently and desperately than ever. But no answer came, and I walked to the edge of a very different black hole, a different kind of darkness, and so began a cycle of doubt.

In the months that followed, my anger grew. Bitterness toward a God who had turned his back on my friend resulted in angry prayers, and those prayers led to heated, one-way shouting matches.

Over spring break of that year, I went down to San Diego to give Kirstin a break as she took a long weekend with her mom and sister. When she picked me up from the airport, we had a tear-filled conversation about the unknown future.

We pulled ourselves together when we got to the house, and I helped Justin and the kids navigate the weekend while Kirstin got some much-needed rest. For four days, I stared Justin's disease in the face and held myself together, thinking I was being strong for my friend.

After returning home, I stood in my living room and looked at a picture of the four of us from our trip to Europe. There we were, all standing and smiling. I lost it.

"Who the hell do you think you are?" I yelled.

"How dare you take away his ability to hold his kids! How dare you take away his ability to hold his wife! How dare you take away his hands, his lifeblood! Weren't his legs enough?

"I thought you were bigger than this! I thought you were powerful!" I screamed.

Out of breath, I lay on the floor of my living room and cried, and my faith crumbled.

Still attending church, I slowly became disengaged. Little desire existed to be a part of anything faith-based, and doubt reigned. Turning to time with my family and music, I attempted to fill the void. Over the next two years, I stuffed my anger and bitterness deep inside. And despite the time we spent together and the many phone calls in between, I left Justin unaware of the internal struggle that was brewing.

During the summer of 2012, Justin and his family visited us

in Idaho. Our week together was crammed with family time as Justin's brother, Ryan, came over with his wife, Tara, and their two children, and Justin's parents drove from nearby Ontario. On Saturday, we had a laughter-filled barbecue and late-night conversation as the adults sat on the back patio under a brilliant moonlit sky. Sunday morning, we loaded up the cars and drove to Eagle Nazarene Church, as we did every Sunday. After the service, Justin and I got involved in an extended conversation with Ed Weaver, the church's associate pastor.

Ed had a history with both of us, dating back more than twenty years to when he was our youth pastor at Ontario First Church of the Nazarene. From the summer after sixth grade through our junior year of high school, Ed had endured our disrespectful behavior and immature antics. It was a welcome change to have a conversation with him as adults, and an opportunity for Ed to catch up on the many happenings in Justin's life a thousand miles away.

Deep in conversation, I was about to see proof of something more. I needed something tangible to counter the doubt and lack of understanding. I didn't know it, but I needed a miracle.

As our discussion came to a close, Ed and Justin continued talking quietly off to the side. In their conversation, I overheard Ed ask Justin, "If you could receive physical healing right now, would you choose it?"

I was certain I knew what Justin's response would be: "Of course!" But Justin looked up at Ed from his wheelchair and said with authority, "No!"

Dumbfounded, all I could think was, *Wait . . . he said no?*

In a moment when time seemed to stand still, it hit me. This wasn't my fight. For the past two years, I had been bitter and angry because the battle I had been fighting was a losing one. My friend was slowly wasting away, and there was nothing being done.

So focused on his apparent need for physical healing, for the miracle, I had failed to recognize what Justin really needed: He needed me to step into the real battle. He needed hands and feet—*my* hands and feet. The miracle had already happened.

That's when I realized that, more often than not, the miracle isn't the absence of struggle, disease, or pain; it is the presence of grace and certainty, the ability to face strife, the unknown, or a slow death, without fear. My obsession with divine intervention had distracted me from the truth that God had already intervened.

We desperately want provision to make sense on our terms—bills paid, food on the table, and sickness taken away—but simply waiting on God and being angry when he doesn't show up the way we want him to is a perverted sense of provision. Make no mistake, I believe that physical healings still happen. But God has made it pretty clear that while he answers prayers, those answers are based on his understanding, not our own; and when it comes to God's provision for the world, we are the front lines. Or at least we should be.

| | |

Being hands and feet to the world is often referred to as a biblical concept, and yet it is never directly referenced in the Bible. However, Jesus paints a very clear picture in Matthew 25 about what it means to be hands and feet to the world around us. Here, Jesus tells the story of the goats and the sheep.

Jesus has returned, and the entire world is gathered at the

foot of his throne. He separates everyone into two groups as a shepherd would separate goats from sheep. The goats go to his left, and he places the sheep on his right. As he addresses those on his right, he invites them to receive their blessing from his Father, and he tells them the reason for their blessing.

"When I was hungry you fed me, and when I was thirsty you gave me something to drink. When I was a stranger you invited me into your homes, and when I was naked you gave me clothes to wear. When I was sick you visited me and took care of me, and when I was in prison you came to me."

Then those on his right ask in confusion, "When did we feed you? When did we give you drink? When did we invite you into our homes? When did we clothe you? When did we tend to you when you were sick or visit you in prison?"

Jesus answers, "Whatever you have done for the least of my brothers, you have done to me."[3]

Over the years, I've discovered that many biblical scholars use this passage to demonstrate a God who chooses, who decides who is in and who is out. But I see a lesson that must not be overlooked. Feed the hungry, give drink to the thirsty, invite the stranger in, clothe the naked, visit the sick, and go to those in prison.

Justin and I have experienced so much provision here on the Camino, and so much before we left home—a wheelchair purchased by others, financial assistance for the trip, shelter when Justin's wheel broke, a welder's skills to repair it, and the push and pull of countless pilgrims. So many things have happened through the hands and feet of others.

Undeniably, we are the front lines of God's provision to the world. If we believe Jesus left his Holy Spirit among us, then we must embrace the fact that He charges us with the very task of loving the world. Loving the world on his terms. Loving the world unconditionally and passionately meeting the needs of others, of those who are broken. We are his hands and feet. We are his provision for the world.

But how often do we see others struggling and take on their cause, raising the battle flag in an effort to fight for them, without knowing what they're fighting for, without knowing what they really need? What I had failed to see was that I had created a battle that Justin wasn't fighting. I was waging war on behalf of my friend, when what he really needed was for me to step into his battle. Not a battle for healing, but a battle for living, a battle for provision. Waiting on a miracle and wrecked by doubt, I had failed to see the little miracles unfolding to my right and to my left.

Every human interaction, every relationship is an opportunity to provide for one another, to provide time, energy, resources, hope, love, compassion, or grace. There is no limit to what we can provide for others, or what others can provide for us.

| | |

By embracing the life he's been given, Justin has provided me with a new perspective, a moment of proof. Life is messy, and the only way I can make it through is to let others carry the burdens I can't. But I have to let go of the safety I find in my own abilities; I have to let go of the reins so I can embrace the provision of others.

Here at the foot of this iron cross in the mountains of northern

Spain, my friend is teaching me yet another lesson. While I have physically pushed him the past several weeks and years, he has slowly, patiently—and perhaps even unknowingly—been pushing me to see that I am capable of more than I think I am. I just have to trust God and his strength instead of my own.

All the pain, doubt, and fear Justin left behind so many years ago is now shining a spotlight on my insecurity. I have been wrestling with what comes next. This journey has changed me, and now I know that I must turn my back on the safety I have known, on the complacent comfort I have taken for granted. I've always felt I had to do everything on my own. There is safety in that. I can control the outcome. But there is so much more out there for me if I trust others to do what I cannot, just as Justin has trusted me to do what he cannot. He needs me to embrace whatever comes next so that we can truly do this together.

Becca's words have stayed with me.

I will be praying for your safety along the journey.

I turn to Justin, and the look in his eyes and the nod of his head tell me he understands what I'm about to do. Stepping over stone after stone, I work my way up the vast expanse of rock until I'm standing next to the post that supports the iron cross. Doubt—in myself, in others, and in God—has kept me from experiencing so many great things for far too long.

As I place the prayer angel on a rock at the base of the pole, I say out loud, "Thank you, Becca. I don't want to be safe anymore."

22

YOU'RE NOT PUSHING

— JUSTIN—

THE MOMENT PATRICK SET his little prayer angel at the foot of the cross, I could see something shift in his eyes.

Sitting here at a late dinner Patrick has made in the kitchen in our albergue, I ask him, "What did you mean today when you said it?"

"When I said what?"

He knows what I'm asking, but he's going to make me say it anyway. "What did you mean by *I don't want to be safe anymore*?"

He looks at me as he cuts my pasta and sausage. "I'm not entirely sure. Still working through it."

After giving me a few bites and taking several of his own, he puts down his fork, leans his head back, and stares at the ceiling, deep in thought. His breathing slows as he gathers his words.

"I don't know what leaving safety behind looks like, but I do know what it's not."

"Okay . . . ," I say, prodding him to continue.

"For me, safety is me. It is what I can do, what I can control.

233

Safety means not allowing outside forces to influence what I can achieve. Pretty flawed thinking, huh?"

"If I thought that way, I would still be at the airport!" I say with a laugh.

After he lifts my cup to my mouth for a drink, I continue. "You have to let people in; you have to take a risk on them. Sometimes they might let you down, but more often than not, they'll surprise you."

The smile on Patrick's face tells me he knows who I'm talking about.

| | |

Our start this morning is a little later than usual. Yesterday's early departure, coupled with our late-night chat, caused us to sleep later than we had intended. This morning, we're the last ones to leave the albergue, and we hit the trail alone.

As Patrick begins pushing me, he's moving slower than normal. Our rest days in León seem forever ago, and Patrick is feeling it in every muscle and every bone.

Yesterday, when he walked back down the mound of stones to where I sat, I knew that whatever the change was, it was permanent. I think he's still working through it today. He is uncharacteristically quiet. I know his calves have started to hurt again and he is definitely in pain, but there seem to be deeper thoughts rattling around in his head.

Today, like many other days, we plan to trek nearly twenty miles to the quaint mountain town of Villafranca del Bierzo. There, we will meet our friends from home, Michael and his sixteen-year-old son, Matthew. They timed their trip to Spain to help us with the last part of our journey, and they'll be with us when we meet up with Joe and Richard at the base of the ascent into O Cebreiro. But first we have to get to Villafranca.

With almost 340 miles behind us, Patrick keeps putting one foot in front of the other. But as we begin to climb another long hill, his gait slows. Soon he's taking ten steps at the most before he is forced to stop and rest because of the pain in his calves. For whatever reason, after twenty-seven days on the Camino, the strain of pushing me up this particular hill is almost too much for him to bear. Our ten-step intervals soon become eight, and eventually drop to five. We aren't even halfway up the hill, and with Patrick's increasing pain and cramping, there's no way we're going to make it the remaining distance.

"Let's stop and go back down to rest," I say. Patrick's lack of protest tells me this is definitely the right decision.

At the bottom of the hill, he stretches his calves and rubs out the knots in an effort to reduce his discomfort. Since walking out the front door of our albergue this morning, we haven't seen a single other pilgrim. Patrick finally sits down on a bench next to my chair, and we begin to discuss what to do next.

"Should we just get a taxi?" Patrick jokes half-heartedly. This is the first time we have seriously considered skipping an entire section of the trail, and we both feel like raising the white flag. For almost an hour, we sit and rest in silence. Though I don't want Patrick to hurt himself, the thought of skipping a section feels like we would be cheating ourselves.

"What do you think?" I ask him.

"I don't like the thought of giving up on this stretch, but we have to get to Villafranca today. I don't know that I can get us there."

After a few more minutes of silence, I ask, "So?"

"I'm not done yet," Patrick says with determination.

"Give it one more shot?"

Patrick nods his head. "One more shot."

| | |

— PATRICK —

Justin's faith in me is flattering, but right now it feels misplaced. I am struggling up this hill just as much as I did an hour ago— maybe more so. My body is covered in sweat, and though my hands feel weak, they are the least of my worries

How much more can my body take? . . . Is this it? . . . Have I reached the end of what I can do?

With every step, my legs feel heavier. The pain in my calves throbs in time with my heartbeat. I just want the pain to stop . . . please make it stop.

More time. I thought I had more time.

I was afraid this would happen, but I thought it wouldn't catch up with me until the very end. Now, it's all I can do to take ten steps before I'm forced to rest. But I have to keep going. I can't stop now. I can't stop here.

Just steady yourself and push through the pain.

The ache spreads to my thighs, and my calves begin to quiver before I can take eight more steps.

Rest . . . just a few minutes of rest.

I decide to keep moving, but after five more steps, the pain is almost unbearable, and the weakness is spreading. I extend my right leg back to stretch my calf muscles. This offers a momentary reprieve from the pain. The slight relief I feel as I stretch my left leg tells me I can keep going.

As we near the point where we turned around last time, I'm down to three or four steps before I have to rest. Justin tries to encourage me.

"One more step. You can do this. Just focus on one more step."

I keep moving, little by little, but after three more steps, I realize I'm done. This is it—my legs won't carry me any farther.

Why is this happening now?

Justin leans back in his chair, eyes closed, and takes a deep breath as he considers our options. I know he isn't disappointed in me, but I'm disappointed in myself. I can't do any more, and we have so far to go. I'm leaning my chest into the handlebars to keep the chair stationary. We hold our position on the hill, not quite ready to head back down, but my legs are done; I can feel it. It has been hours and not a single other pilgrim has passed by.

My body is beginning to shake with fatigue when I hear footsteps drawing closer behind us. Each footfall is a little louder than the last. I'm almost afraid to look, afraid that I'm hearing things.

A beautiful voice with an Australian accent washes over me like water.

"Can I help?"

"Yes!" Justin and I reply in unison.

Standing next to us is a young woman in her late twenties with a brown pack on her back. She's wearing a black hat to keep the sun off her head, and dark sunglasses hide her eyes, but there is so much warmth in her smile.

"I'm Victoria. What can I do?" she asks confidently.

I grab the nylon harness and hand it to her.

"We need you to pull. Are you up to it?"

Nodding, she follows my instructions for anchoring the nylon webbing to Justin's wheelchair and steps into the harness. With a fresh set of legs and all the strength I can muster, we finish the climb.

"Thanks for the help!" Justin says as we reach the top of the hill.

"You're welcome," Victoria says with a smile. "Where did you guys start?"

"St. Jean," I reply.

"Oh my! You've been at this a while then."

A stretch of flat trail allows Victoria and me to catch our breath and start a conversation.

"So, what do you do back home?" I ask her.

"I work for Scope in the UK, actually. It's an organization similar to your Muscular Dystrophy Association."

Of all the pilgrims to come alongside to help us, we get Victoria, who works with people with disabilities! As we continue to march down the trail, Justin shares details about his disease, life at home, and previous travels abroad.

Victoria's help has made the pain in my calves tolerable, but now I'm afraid she'll think we no longer need her help and move on.

"How far are you planning on going today?" she shouts from the front. The red nylon stretches taut as she leans into it, pulling hard up another short hill.

"Villafranca," Justin replies. "We have some friends who are meeting us there to help on the climb to O Cebreiro."

"Can I walk with you guys? I'm headed there too."

| | |

Michael and Matthew Turner arrive safely in Villafranca, and when we get to town, we meet up with Christie, Tiffanie, and

Claudia, as well. We have become accustomed to the ebb and flow of pilgrims as they've come in and out of our lives for the past few weeks, and it feels good to see these girls again. We exchange hugs and introduce them all to the Turners.

After dinner, before we return to our albergue, Justin gets Claudia's attention and says, "Thank you for sending us your journal entry . . . for sharing what you experienced."

She smiles and replies, "I thought it was important for you two to know the impact that day had on me. So, thank you."

She hugs Justin again and then turns to me. As I give her another hug, I tell her, "I hope you will someday realize the impact you've had on us, what you've done for us. There are no words . . . but thank you."

| | |

The next morning, after a good night's sleep, my calves are still sore. At breakfast with Michael and Matthew, I spend a good thirty minutes stretching, but it doesn't seem to help much. We head out to meet with the girls before we begin the day's westward march.

Today, our initial destination is the small town of Vega de Valcarce, about ten and a half miles up the road, where we plan to meet up with Joe and Richard, the young men from Boise who offered to help us on the climb to O Cebreiro. Though my calves continue to hurt like crazy and I have to stretch them every time we stop, I still manage to push Justin the majority of the time, with some help from our crew: Christie, Tiffanie, Claudia, Michael, and Matthew. Despite my ongoing discomfort, we make good time and arrive in Vega de Valcarce a little after eleven o'clock in the morning.

Just as we had planned several weeks earlier, Joe and Richard are waiting for us at a small café. Our number has grown by two more for the steep climb to O Cebreiro. I hope it's enough help.

Parking Justin next to Joe on the patio of the café, I notice Jess sitting with a number of pilgrims I haven't seen before, all with their backpacks resting at their feet. It's not uncommon to see other pilgrims when we stop for lunch, but something feels different here. Some of these strangers eye me with curiosity as I lock Justin's brakes, unclip the harness that secures me to his chair, and head next door to a small store to buy some fruit and refill our water bottles.

Back at the café, Justin introduces Michael and Matthew to Joe and Richard. Together, with friends new and old, we eat a quick lunch in preparation for heading up the mountain. When everyone is finished eating, we begin to gather our things. But as we stand up to leave, everyone else in the café stands up as well.

Justin turns to Joe and asks, "Who are all these people?"

"They're here to help!" he replies. "As they walked by and asked if we're headed to O Cebreiro, we told them, 'Not yet, we're waiting to help Justin and Patrick up the mountain. Justin's in a wheelchair.' Each one of them said they would like to help."

What started out as two young men in Burgos offering assistance has now become a group of about a dozen pilgrims, many of them strangers, ready to make sure we make it to the top of our final mountain pass.

A woman in her fifties approaches Justin and me.

"Hi, I'm Julie."

Her accent sounds familiar, but I ask just to be sure.

"Where are you from?"

"New Zealand."

"Jane, from Ireland," another woman says as she waves and smiles from the table behind Julie.

A third woman approaches, and as she reaches out her hand, Joe introduces her.

"This is Xenia."

"I'm from Belgium," she adds before we can ask.

As I release the brakes on Justin's chair, Joe steps up close to me, puts a finger in my face, and says with authority, "You're not pushing! At least not for a while."

Taking the safety harness out of my hands, he wraps it around his own waist and takes hold of the handlebars. It's clear there's no point in arguing.

As the group begins to move toward the Camino trail, for the first time in more than 360 miles, I'm not at the helm of Justin's chair. Sure, there have been times when Team Ted or Christie or others have pushed, but I've always been right there, close enough to jump in if needed. But as Joe takes off with a spring in his step and the other pilgrims fall in with his pace, in a matter of minutes, I find myself several hundred feet behind, watching one of the hardest and yet most amazing parts of our journey unfold. This group of twelve people, including a number of complete strangers, has stepped in to do what I can no longer do on my own.

Tears stream down my face as the journey finally forces me to fully embrace the help of others—just as Justin's disease has forced him to do in so much of his life.

This is so very hard, but so beautiful.

Our journey began as a physical one. For days on end, I have pushed Justin. Now, I'm finding, he's pushing me—in ways I didn't know I needed; in ways I doubt he is fully aware of. But it keeps happening. Just a few days ago, at the base of Cruz de Ferro, I committed to letting go of fear, letting go of the safety I have clung to, fleeing from the complacency that has been filling my life. I felt a shift in my psyche, and my soul began to fill up as I thought about what walking in faith instead of fear would look like.

Though Justin has breathed encouraging words into my ears ever since our initial climb up the Pyrenees, it hasn't been his words that have pushed me as much as who he is. Every day, I have watched him embrace my help and the help of others, and those days have all led to this moment. By letting go of control and welcoming the strength of others to do what he cannot, Justin has been pushing me to let go of my need for control, to let go of comfort, to let go of safety, to let go of fear, and to embrace a life lived in faith, with others at my side.

Watching this tribe come together around Justin, I understand how one can lead with faith. By placing his faith in those around him, who are capable of doing things he can't, who are capable of taking him places he never could reach on his own, Justin's faith in us is pushing each of us to do the same. Just as Joe is pushing for Justin, his words at the outset—*you're not pushing*—let me know he is also doing it for me. I have led the charge, or pushed, in every aspect of our journey. But now I see it—sometimes the best way to lead is to get out of the way. I have to place my faith in the love these people are actively giving us. I have to relinquish control to the hands and feet that God has laid in our path. I have to place my hope in the people he has provided, in much the same way Justin has placed his faith in me.

| | |

— JUSTIN —

Surrounded by friends and strangers, we have made our way to the base of the trail leading up to O Cebreiro. For this most recent section of the Camino, we've been largely on paved roads, but now we have the option of a dirt trail leading up the mountain.

Everyone asks me, "Road or trail?" Both are steep, and I consider the road for a moment. But who am I kidding? We haven't taken the easier route once.

"Life is never easy!" I reply. "Let's take the trail!"

We aren't on the dirt-and-rock path for very long before we encounter a steep incline littered with stair-step stones and large rocks. Up ahead, we can see other pilgrims struggling up the steep mountain path—and they don't have a 250-pound wheelchair to contend with.

As the trail grows more uneven and rocky, it soon becomes obvious that the only way up is for me to be carried.

Christie is first to vocalize what we need to do. "We are going to have to carry Justin, just like we did outside of Burgos," she says to Patrick.

"We need six people," Patrick yells. "We're going to carry Justin in his chair."

Everyone is ready to jump in and help with the carry, but Patrick and Christie give directions to the first six volunteers. As I am hoisted into the air, they march ahead.

For several miles, the trail requires me to be carried, and for several miles the various pilgrims rotate in and out of the different positions. Groans from straining muscles and sore bodies can be heard all around me, as everyone is stepping over large stones and up the uneven stairs of dirt, rock, and roots. Despite the struggle, no one is giving less than one hundred percent.

While six people carry me in my chair, others carry the extra backpacks and walking sticks. Pilgrims continue to rotate in and out as we gradually make progress, and I find myself at the center of a remarkable human symphony. Before I know it, new people join the mix, and I meet Odei from Barcelona and another young man from Ireland. Each of these people are soon drenched in sweat, have sore muscles, and suffer from blistered feet. Hands, arms, and calves are cramping as the team lifts, pushes, pulls, and carries me with every ounce of energy they possess. I can't help, but I can definitely encourage.

"You guys have got this!" I yell. "You are all amazing!"

The trail gets steeper.

"Keep moving, keep moving."

Soon, Christie calls out from behind me, "I need a break."

I shout out to the crew, "Christie needs a break, can some-one—"

Before I can finish, Julie from New Zealand is at my side, ready to step in.

Despite the struggle, every face is full of joy, a joy that comes from giving of themselves, and I am at the center of it all. I can't stop smiling. They say it is better to give than to receive, but right now the gift I am receiving is incredible, indescribable. This is one of the most humbling experiences of my entire life, and I wouldn't trade it for anything.

Back home, I have an inner circle of people whom I trust enough to do all the things I can no longer do. Kirstin and Patrick are the two at the very center of this circle. I didn't go into my marriage thinking that one day my wife would have to feed me and brush my teeth. I never thought that one day I would ask my best friend to hold a urinal steady so I could pee, or wipe my backside because I could no longer hold toilet paper or reach. But this is now my reality. The first time I asked Patrick to help me use the bathroom, I hated it. I felt like I was a burden. Part of me was back on my front porch, questioning God. But Patrick, just like Kirstin, has never thought twice. He has always been happy to do whatever needs to be done. Just knowing that he can make my life a little easier brings him joy—the same joy I see on the faces of these people who are now carrying me up this incredibly steep mountain trail.

Over the years, my pride has slowly been pushed aside as I have embraced all the things I can no longer do on my own, all the things others now have to do for me.

I'm not sure who said it—or even where I heard it—but there's a fundamental truth that has stayed with me over the years: "When you deny someone the opportunity to help you, you deny them joy in life."

I've had to embrace a lot of help over the past several years, and I have seen this truth play out in the lives of others time and time again. There is so much joy in giving, in helping others. A joy God intended for all of us to experience.

Patrick has always been one to give relentlessly, but it is time he learns to receive.

As we continue the struggle of the climb, the group has a break from carrying me, and now they are able to just push, pull, and drag me up the mountain. Soon we get a view of the valley where we started, far below us. Laughter and words of encouragement rise from our group as we begin passing through small mountain villages.

"Would it be easier if I got up and walked?" I yell at Joe.

He and Richard begin to laugh as he shouts back at me, "Yes, yes it would!"

In spite of the strain of the climb, everyone is laughing now. Town residents come out of their homes to see what has caused the ruckus invading their quiet, little hamlets.

By the time we reach the top of the trail, where it reunites with the mountain road, we are greeted by two volunteer police officers in a bright yellow truck. They had heard about our climb and were waiting for us on the road.

No words are exchanged, except a gruff but sincere *"¡Buen Camino!"* as one of the officers grabs the red nylon harness at the front of my chair and begins to pull me the rest of the way into O Cebreiro, while his partner drives the truck behind us with lights flashing.

When we finally make it to the top, all I can do is look around at the people who have given so much for me today. As we gather together for a photo, "thank you" doesn't seem like nearly enough after all they've done, but it's all I can give.

"Thanks, everyone!" I shout as Mike prepares to take the picture.

"On the count of three, say *'¡Buen Camino!'*" Mike yells to the group.

"¡BUEN CAMINO!"

I may not be able to feed myself, shower myself, or go to the bathroom by myself. I may not be able to hug my daughter, play catch with my boys, or hold my wife's hand as we walk along a beach at sunset. But today, through the power, love, and sacrifice of others, *I climbed a mountain.*

| | |

— PATRICK —

Sitting in his wheelchair with his back to me, Justin watches the sun set beyond the vast valley below us. Deep in thought, he doesn't know I'm here.

We have officially entered the lush region of Galicia, and the oranges and yellows of the sky bleed into the vast expanse of green stretching out to the west. Less than one hundred miles to Santiago.

The past several days have been filled with so much self-discovery. I walked away from Cruz de Ferro with open hands, having given up fear disguised as safety, but I had no idea what this kind of change in my life would mean or how I would navigate it. I just knew I had to do it. I needed to do it for my wife, for my kids, and for me.

Earlier in the day, when we were resting at the top of one of our ascents, Justin and I had a moment to ourselves.

"How do you do it?" I asked.

"How do I do what?"

"How have you let go of so much safety and lived such a full life in spite of this disease?" I've known Justin my whole life, and I felt as if I should know the answer to this question, but I didn't.

"Letting go wasn't really a choice," Justin said, "but living a full life is a decision I make every time I let others help me do things I can't do on my own."

Here on top of the mountain, as I stand behind my friend, I'm beginning to realize how often I tend to overcomplicate things. I'm not being physically forced to let go of safety, but if I'm going to value my wife, my kids, and my relationships as much as I want

247

to, letting go is the only choice I have. God has shown me what a powerful gift I can give others by simply loving through my actions, through being his hands and feet. But openly and graciously receiving this same love from others is a whole new kind of beauty, a new kind of freedom—a freedom I witnessed today as my fellow pilgrims carried Justin up this mountain.

If I'm going to embrace a life of faith, I must embrace the gifts of provision that God gives to me. I must embrace the help of my wife, my neighbors, my friends—and even complete strangers. I must welcome the helping hands of people I've only just met, like Victoria, the crew of pilgrims who hauled us up the mountain today, and friends like Ted, Michael, and Matthew, who have flown across the ocean to help us chase a dream. To live a life of faith, I must no longer trust solely in my own strength; I must let go of safety and learn to trust the strength of the people God surrounds me with.

I walk up to Justin as he continues to look out from atop this beautiful mountain landscape. Hearing my approach, he looks up at me, and a smile spreads across his face.

"Can you believe we made it?" he asks.

"Yeah, I can."

23

PROVISION

— JUSTIN —

WITH LESS THAN seventy miles to go before we reach Santiago de Compostela, both Patrick and I are beyond weary. But the remarkable events on the climb to O Cebreiro have us reeling in waves of gratitude and wonderment. Several days have passed since our many friends pushed, pulled, carried, and dragged me up the mountain pass, and many of them have gone ahead. Now it's the two of us, along with our friends Michael and Matthew, as we leave the town of Sarria on our way to Portomarín.

Pilgrims who walk the Camino carry a pilgrim's "passport" known as the *credencial del peregrino*. This document allows pilgrims to stay at the albergues along the Camino and serves as proof of their travel. Whenever pilgrims stay in a town, they can receive a stamp from a local church, albergue, restaurant, or hotel. The stamp on their passport proves they passed through the specific town or city. When pilgrims reach Santiago de Compostela, they can present this collection of stamps at the Pilgrim's Reception Office. Once the credenciales have been examined for appropriate stamps and dates, the pilgrims are presented with their *compostela*, a certificate of completion of their journey. Pilgrims must walk at least the last one hundred kilometers (sixty-two miles) of the Camino, or ride the last two hundred kilometers on bicycle, in order to receive this certificate.

The town of Sarria lies 116 kilometers east of Santiago, which makes it a fairly major access point for the Camino. Many choose to start their pilgrimage here because it's just far enough away from Santiago for them to earn a compostela. With so many people trekking this shorter distance to the cathedral in Santiago, it makes for some congestion, and now we're even seeing families walking with their children.

There are so many stories represented by each person we meet—some are filled with joy, some with sorrow, and most with a combination of the two; but each person is finding something here. For many it is friendship, peace, healing, or connection with God. Whatever it is, it's beautiful.

| | |

For the past several days, Michael and Matthew have been pulling or pushing more often in an effort to give Patrick a break. Still, we've had to stop fairly frequently so Patrick can stretch out his leg muscles, but the pain never seems to subside. He has been more willing to let others help, and though I know he welcomes the break from the strain on his legs, the real reason is a new perspective.

Yesterday, we talked a lot about what comes next in life.

"I'm going back," Patrick said when I asked about his job at the hospital, "but I'm not staying for long."

Though I hadn't expected this, I wasn't surprised.

"So, what are you going to do instead?" I asked.

"I'm not sure yet, but we'll do it together."

| | |

— PATRICK —

My mental and spiritual shift over the past week has challenged me in many ways. Time and time again, we have had the help we needed, and every time, it was help we didn't ask for. For as long as I can remember, I have struggled with asking others for assistance. But the challenge of accepting help that is freely offered opened my eyes to a deeper struggle. I haven't just struggled to *ask*, I have struggled to *receive*. Over the past few days, though, I've seen a beauty in receiving that I didn't know existed. A beauty I am about to witness yet again.

We're now facing a short climb through a forested area just west of Sarria. The towering trees seem to have equally large roots growing up through the soil below us. Getting Justin's chair over these roots is more than Michael, Matthew, and I can handle.

"¡Buen Camino!" we hear echoed in a chorus of voices as a group of cyclists passes to our left on a narrow pathway worn by many years and millions of tires. When the last cyclist makes it to the top of the hill, we see her stop and look back at us. Recognizing our struggle, she yells something in Italian to her fellow pilgrims and points down the hill. Before we quite know what's happening, we're surrounded by eight men and women in cycling togs, and in a matter of two minutes, we have covered a distance equal to what we had managed over the previous half hour.

Until the hill climb up to O Cebreiro, every bit of help we received from other pilgrims had me feeling uncomfortable. On the surface, I was fine with it, but my pride was hiding just below my expressions of gratitude, and my ego was telling me I should be doing all of this for Justin and doing it all by myself. Even the help Ted poured out on the Pyrenees—and for so many days after—left a bit of a sting to my pride.

For years, I've been open and vulnerable with Justin and Donna about my weaknesses, but I hadn't ever embraced sacrificing my pride and receiving help from others until I stood back and watched a group of people do what I could not. How much joy have I robbed from others with my resistance to receiving help? How many things have I failed to achieve because I had to do it all on my own?

Today, accepting help feels different. As Justin, Michael, Matthew, and I thank the Italian cyclists for their assistance, I'm not at all uncomfortable. My ego isn't whispering lies, telling me I should have been able to do it on my own. No pride clouds the beauty of their assistance. With the condition my body is in and the distance we have left to cover, I have finally embraced my limitations and am beginning to recognize that my vulnerability is my greatest strength.

| | |

— JUSTIN —

Patrick and I are fortunate to have a friendship that has endured so long. We have helped each other in many ways. But no matter how much help I have offered Patrick, or how much he has given me, our relationship is a dynamic interaction between two people. This means there are two decisions that must be made in order for it to work. The strength and energy we can effectively give each other is directly proportional to the willingness of the other to receive it. It's no different out here on the trail.

I face challenge after challenge as this disease continues to take more of my ability to use my body. In spite of this, I strive to live a life of adventure and make the most of every day. But living this way requires utter vulnerability. Because the list of things I can do on my own is so much shorter than the list of those I can't, I have to acknowledge my limitations and allow others to step in and do those things for me. No matter how much help Patrick offers me, he can't help me if I refuse it. When I choose pride over vulnerability, I find that relying on my own strength makes me weak.

When I laid everything on the table back in 2012 and proposed the idea of tackling the Camino, Patrick's response—"I'll push you!"—would have meant nothing if I hadn't been willing to accept his help and admit that I couldn't do it all on my own. I didn't realize this was a lesson Patrick needed to learn, but he echoed this sentiment yesterday when he told me, "I have accepted the fact that I can't do any of this on my own."

Before we left St. Jean Pied de Port on June 3 and ascended the Pyrenees Mountains, I had accepted my limits and embraced not being able to make the pilgrimage without help. If I had never accepted my limitations and allowed others to help, I would still be sitting in my living room watching PBS. The truth is, something beautiful happens when I invite others into my weaknesses. I don't mean just the hard moments in life, like the death of a loved one, addiction to pornography, or not being able to care for myself. I mean *everything*. When I invite others into everything I am, no weakness is too great to overcome.

I don't think Patrick ever truly thought he could get me all the way to Santiago on his own, but he certainly hadn't accepted the prospect that he couldn't. At least not until recently. By letting go of the things he knows he cannot do alone, like getting me up to O Cebreiro, he is offering me even more, and he is offering more to other pilgrims on the trail. They were able to help, and I was able to climb a mountain because he finally let go. I'm convinced that if he had continued to push through the pain in his calves rather than let others help as much as they have, our Camino would have ended several days before now. He had to completely relinquish control so others could do what he could not. Just as I've lost strength in my body but have discovered a freedom I didn't know when I could walk, Patrick had to lose the strength in his legs in order to discover the freedom that exists in resting in the strength of others.

Today is Jasper's last day on the film crew. He has filmed so much of this journey, but he has one request before he leaves.

"Can I push today? I want to push for a bit!"

Patrick unclips the safety harness and steps aside so Jasper can take the handlebars. Jasper's face lights up as he says, "I have wanted to do this ever since St. Jean!"

While Jasper pushes, Patrick and I talk a great deal about the Basque man who affectionately slapped my cheek so many days ago.

"A stranger in the middle of the Pyrenees has turned into a bit of a prophet."

"Yeah! I wonder if he will ever understand the power of his words?" Patrick muses.

"I hope so, but do any of us ever know the power of our words?"

"No, I guess not. That's why we should make sure they are filled with hope."

It has been exactly one month since we heard the man shout, "The impossible is possible!" And we have seen more examples of this truth than we could ever imagine. Our journey has led Patrick and me over three mountain ranges, through days of self-exploration and discovery, and into the arms of strangers waiting to help us in ways we didn't know we needed.

What an experience.

| | |

— PATRICK —

Two days have passed since the cyclists outside of Sarria helped us, and we are headed today to the town of Arzúa. Michael and Matthew have continued to push and pull whenever needed, and Claudia has rejoined us. Unfortunately, my need for help has been often. I have required their assistance more and more each day. Right now, I'm lying on my belly on the side of the trail, with my face in the damp grass, while Claudia attempts to work out the cramps in my calves. My legs have been so problematic, we have had to literally stop on the side of the trail while she uses her thumbs to knead away at the knots running from the backs of my knees all the way to my ankles. Despite the pain in my legs and the tears in my eyes, I remind myself we are two days from Santiago.

I guess the impossible really is possible.

Because of Justin's audacious goal of traveling five hundred miles through Spain in a wheelchair and his willingness to be completely vulnerable throughout the entire process, I and many others have discovered things we didn't think were possible—feats of strength, feats of mental fortitude, and feats of emotional and spiritual breakthrough.

Without Justin's vision, his willingness to pursue that vision, and his recognition that the only way his dream could be realized was through the power, strength, and will of others—the provision of others—we never would have known what we were capable of.

God has given both of us so much throughout our lives, but the Camino has served as a tangible reminder of this provision. Maybe the provision Justin has received is more noticeable than it is for many on the trail—he needs someone to get him out of bed, dress him, put on his shoes, feed him, shower him, brush his teeth, comb his hair, and help him use the restroom. God has given me provision through a friend who trusts me enough to let me do all those things for him; by teaching me that I can't do everything on my own, that I must surrender myself to the strength others have to offer. I must place my faith in the many people who have pushed and pulled when I could not, who continue to push and pull when I cannot.

This journey has done many things for me, but perhaps the most important is the lesson God has taught me about his provision. This provision can take the form of trust, vulnerability, accountability, intimacy, pursuing one another, and moments of Sabbath. It means trusting others enough to let them do things for me; being vulnerable to the point of letting them carry a load I'm too weak to bear; allowing someone to hold me to a higher standard; being intimate to the point of allowing others to know all of me and realizing they still love me; letting others pursue time with me, rest in my presence, and keep me close.

Provision can be so many things—even an ancient trail through northern Spain.

There is an excitement growing inside me as I think about how to apply the lessons I've learned in this next chapter of life. But as excited as I am about what comes next, it pales in comparison to the anticipation of reaching our final destination. In just two days, our wives will be waiting for us at the base of the cathedral in Santiago.

24

A BEAUTIFUL WAY TO START

— PATRICK —

Yesterday ended with a hill into Arzúa. Matthew had pulled much of the day while Michael and I took turns behind Justin's chair, but as rain began to fall and we added *wet* to tired, hungry, and sore, another new pilgrim came along and asked if he could push.

Tema, our new friend, strapped in behind Justin and powered the wheelchair up the hill to where we would spend the night. After seeing us to the door of our albergue, Tema continued on to meet up with some fellow pilgrims, but not before he asked if he could join us tomorrow.

"Of course!" Justin said as Tema walked away.

After enjoying a quiet dinner with Michael and Matthew, we abused yet another office chair at the albergue so Justin could take a shower.

Today, Tema is with us again, and because of his assistance, coupled with the many days of helping hands from others, my legs feel almost normal. In addition to Tema, we have Michael, Matthew, Claudia, and the film crew (now minus Jasper) accompanying us. Our destination is a small hamlet called Brea, where we have an invitation to stay at a pension (guesthouse). A gentleman named Colin reached out to us on Facebook, offering to arrange a place for us to stay on our final night before reaching Santiago. We plan to spend the evening resting so we can get to the cathedral tomorrow with the sun still at our backs.

For the past thirty-three days and almost five hundred miles, we have been blessed by so many like Tema. The sense of community and connection with each person we have met, and the love we have received from those who have come from our hometown to help, have made for an experience so rich that we are reluctant to see it come to an end. But we are eager to see our wives. It has been more than a month since I last held Donna's hand, kissed her lips, or felt the warmth of her embrace.

Bittersweet is the only way I can describe the thoughts and feelings coursing through our hearts and souls as our Camino draws to a close. When I glance over at Tema, who is now pushing Justin, I see the two of them are deep in conversation.

| | |

— JUSTIN —

Tema is a thirty-eight-year-old police officer from Madrid. As we talk, I discover that he and I share the same birthday—July 12, 1975. We have a natural connection, and while he pushes, he tells me about the grief he is experiencing from a failed relationship. Much of his reason for being on the Camino is an attempt to make sense of his life, like so many others we have met.

When we stop to rest, Tema's smile is bright and there is joy in his eyes. He tells me how the pain in his life is always easier to deal with when he helps others, when he invests in the lives of others. It is not a selfish act, but I understand that Tema isn't pushing only for Patrick or me; he's also pushing for himself. He has embraced the fundamental truth that we are meant to live life together and carry one another's burdens. By pushing me, even if only for a little while, Tema is allowing Patrick and me to help shoulder his burden and ease his pain.

When we arrive at a small side street leading from the Camino trail to our destination for the day, it's still early, and Tema decides to continue on to Santiago. He gives me an intense hug. "I want to give you something for what you have given me," he says with tears in his eyes. As he lays a small watercolor painting in my lap, he grips my shoulders and says, "Thank you!"

I look down at his depiction of rolling hills through Basque country and am reminded of how far we've come.

"Thank you, Tema!" I say as he turns and waves good-bye. Though our time together has been brief, I feel humbled and grateful to have met him and to have shared conversations of life, love, and faith.

Patrick pushes me up the short road to Pension The Way, a spacious white stucco house with a red tile roof set amid an expansive lawn enclosed by a low stone wall and hedges. We are now fifteen miles from our final destination. Only one more night before we're reunited with our wives.

Colin welcomes us in and introduces us to the owners, Tony and Roger, two Englishmen who open their beautiful home from the beginning of May to the end of October each year for pilgrims seeking rest before the final trek into Santiago. They show us around the house and help each member of our group find a room to store their packs and rest their feet.

Patrick and I are given the largest room downstairs. After shedding our backpacks, we head into the backyard of this private estate to spend some time with our gracious hosts. The yard is large and open, with trees and flower beds bordering the lawn. The back of the house faces south, so almost the entire yard is bathed in light, but a small covered porch offers protection from the intense rays. After nearly four hours with the early July sun beating down on my shoulders, I'm ready for some shade.

Directly off the covered patio, on the south side of the home, a long table is set with plates and silverware, ready for the dinner we will share in a few hours. As Patrick and I chat with Roger and Colin, we feel at home. Amid plenty of laughter, we trade stories about the Camino—and even find time for a nap in the shade.

The traditional English dinner is reminiscent of the many communal meals we have shared along the way. Roasted chicken, homemade bread, fresh salad, and pumpkin soup are a welcome change from weeks of bocadillos and Spanish tortillas. Pilgrims from the US, England, France, South America, and Ireland sit around the table. We share food, wine, and community. I am ready to see my wife, but I'm not ready to leave these people, to leave this way of living.

| | |

As our final day of walking dawns bright and clear, we have fifteen miles to go before we reach the square outside the Cathedral of Santiago de Compostela, fifteen miles until we see our wives for the first time in forty days. Before we left Idaho, we had arranged for them to meet us in Santiago. They will be in the square when we arrive. The pull to continue the Camino experience is strong, but the desire to see the women who have loved us and supported us throughout this crazy endeavor is far more powerful.

For the first twelve miles, Patrick pushes me, with Michael, Matthew, and Claudia at our sides. Jess, Christie, John, Lynda, Richard, and Joe have all gone ahead to complete their Caminos.

Three miles from our destination, we arrive at the monument of Monte do Gozo, where two towering statues of pilgrims face west, pointing the way to Santiago. From here we get our first glimpse of the three spires atop the magnificent cathedral in town. Three more miles and we will have completed the five-hundred-mile journey so many people told us was impossible. Three more miles and we will say good-bye to this pilgrimage. Three more miles and we will be in the arms of our wives.

As we continue to work our way toward the center of the city, Michael, Matthew, and Claudia go on ahead. Soon Patrick and I are alone on this last stretch. Each street we cross brings us one step closer, but the city is busy with foot traffic. Navigating around the many pedestrians, we can now see the cathedral ahead of us and to our left. Directly in front of us, a number of pilgrims take the steps leading to the square at the cathedral's base.

These steps force us to change direction, and we take an alternate road leading down to Praza do Obradoiro, the large square outside the Cathedral of Santiago de Compostela. The street ends as it opens up to the plaza, and as we draw near the square, we see hundreds of pilgrims and tourists sitting or reclining along the perimeter, while others have gathered along the smooth stones that make a path to the center of the square.

Not knowing what to expect, we enter the plaza and are greeted by an eruption of applause. Chills go down my spine, and adrenaline flows in my veins.

We made it. We actually made it.

Joe, Richard, Christie, and Tiffanie are here, and as we work our way further into the square, we see more faces we recognize. Amid so many friends, many unfamiliar faces are also smiling at us, and everyone is clapping their hands. Bodies continue to part as we get nearer to the middle of the square, and all we can think is, *Where are our wives?*

Finally, we see them, standing at the center of the plaza. I can feel emotion welling in my chest as tears fill my eyes. I don't know what heaven will be like, but I am guessing today is a glimpse of what we will experience. There are so many familiar faces of pilgrims who have gone before, staring back at us, celebrating our arrival. So many hands and hearts that have helped us along the way. I am thankful for every person in this square, known or unknown to me.

Patrick's pace quickens as he sees Donna and Kirstin. They begin to run toward us, their eyes filled with light. When Kirstin reaches me, she bends down and wraps her arms around my shoulders. Tears of joy flow from both of us. For so long, I have missed her smile, her voice, her laughter, and her touch.

"You made it!" she says into my ear. "I have missed you so much."

"Me too. I love you!"

"I love you."

When Kirstin finally lets go, she turns to Patrick and gives him an embrace filled with heartfelt gratitude. Donna wraps her arms around me with tears in her eyes.

"I told you I would keep him safe," I say with a smile.

"I knew you would."

| | |

— PATRICK —

So many faces, new and old, surround us as we hold our wives for the first time in more than a month. When I finally let Donna go, she looks at me and places her hands on the sides of my face. The corners of her eyes curl up as she smiles.

"Oh how I've missed you," she says.

"I love you so much!" I whisper because my voice is weak with emotion. But once isn't enough. "I love you so much!"

I turn to welcome the arms of Kirstin. "It's so good to see you," I tell her.

We both have tears in our eyes as she smiles and says, "Thank you!"

Those two words are so full of gratitude and love; nothing else needs to be said.

After exchanging more hugs with friends and strangers alike, we introduce Donna and Kirstin to our fellow pilgrims. For the next few minutes, Joe, Richard, Tiffanie, Jess, Claudia, Christie, Julie, Jane, and many others exchange embraces with our wives. Finally, we're ready to head to our hotel rooms for much-needed showers and time to rest in fresh, clean beds.

Later in the afternoon, the four of us set out to explore the city with Michael and Matthew. As we wander the streets around the cathedral, we see so many familiar faces, and we begin to make plans for one more communal meal with our new friends before we all go our separate ways.

At dinner, we take over the patio area of a small restaurant near our hotel. Terry, Mike, and Robin join us, and we all laugh and tell stories about our Camino. Claudia and Jess are soon engrossed in conversation with our wives, while Christie and Tiffanie smile as they soak in the sense of community that surrounds us all. Michael and Matthew get to know some of these people a little better as we eat, and Joe and Richard make sure everyone's glasses are full of wine. There are so many faces, and yet they are just a handful of all who have made this journey possible—a journey on which I have pushed my best friend five hundred miles across Spain and he has pushed me into a new way of life.

An odd mixture of joy and grief fills my chest as Michael stands and gives a toast to our journey and to the friends surrounding us. A toast to friends new and old, a toast to community, a toast to love as God intended it.

| | |

This morning, we collected our compostelas from the Pilgrim's Office, proof of our five hundred-mile journey. Several of the passport officials had trouble believing we had come all this way in a wheelchair.

Now, sitting in the cathedral as the mass draws to a close, Justin, Kirstin, Donna, and I are captivated by the Botafumeiro, a massive brass censer suspended by a rope-and-pulley system from the ceiling high above. When a team of monks pulls on the rope, the censer swings high above our heads, like a pendulum, as fragrant smoke fills the air in the cathedral. Watching it swing back and forth draws me deep into thought. It is almost hypnotizing, like watching the flames of a campfire lick the night air. This is a time of reflection, a time of gratitude. This mass, this final *amen*, brings a sense of closure to our Camino while filling me with anticipation for what comes next.

It is the end of one journey and the beginning of another.

What a beautiful way to start.

ACKNOWLEDGMENTS

WE WOULD LIKE TO EXPRESS our gratitude to so many people who have seen us through the writing of this book and who have made this journey possible.

To the Turners, Hamptons, Greens, Bryants, Martins, and Kluksdals: You are our church. Thank you for sharing every Monday night on the patio with us. Long live MNOP!

Thank you to Chris Karcher and Terry Parish from emota, Inc. for cataloging the journey, making our film possible, and for having faith in us since day one.

Thank you to Mike McLeod, Jasper Newton, and Robin Romera for your incredible work ethic and amazing eyes. You captured truly beautiful moments on camera.

Theresa McLeod, you are the most amazing mother/sister/friend.

Scott Hancock, thank you for being such a champion for love and light.

Angela Scheff and Chris Ferebee, you have been unbelievable in this process. Thank you for giving us a chance and for being the best literary agents anyone could hope for.

Seth Haines, we are forever in your debt. Your editorial skills have made this book so much more than we could have hoped for.

Sarah Atkinson and the entire Tyndale Momentum team, thank you for your faith in us and in our story. You have been incredible partners. Thank you for bringing this book to life.

Catherine Oliva, thank you for all the work on the speaking front. Your work has made so much of this possible. Thank you for being an incredible speaking agent and friend.

To the countless friends who have walked by our side on this crazy journey, we love you. Thank you, Ted and Amee Hardy, and Michael and Matthew Turner, for your help on the trail. Thank you, Julie Turner and Amee Hardy, for letting your husbands accompany our shenanigans.

To all who have helped support the film and our endeavors, you are too many to name here, but you are loved and appreciated.

Our incredible fellow pilgrims: Joe, Richard, Christie, Claudia, John, Bernie, Lynda, Jess, Tiffanie, Ray, Julie, Jane, Tema, and so many others—there is no way we could have made it without you. Thank you for loving us!

— FROM PATRICK —

Where to begin? I am indebted to so many amazing individuals who have influenced who I am—and will continue to.

Ed Castledine, thank you for pushing me out of my comfort zone and being an incredible mentor.

Howard King, thank you for your endless wisdom and patience with me. You have influenced many of my decisions with your perspective on life.

To my parents, Jerry and Karyn Gray, thank you for raising me, thank you for being my mom and dad, and thank you for your love, support, and prayer. I appreciate all the guidance over the years.

Jeff Gray and Susan Pennington, your words of encouragement have meant more than you know. Kilian Gray, I will never forget the day you brought me a manila envelope full of your savings to help us on our journey. Thank you for such incredible generosity.

Jennifer and Dean Coon, you both believed in this journey from the start. I am grateful for your love and support. James, thank you for the joy and energy you bring to our family.

Michael Gray, thank you for the countless hours on the phone. Your friendship means more than I could ever put into words. Kathleen Gray, thank you for sharing him with me. Lila and Sophie, you are both wonderful in so many ways.

Kenoyer clan, you all have been a remarkable extended family. Doug, Megan, Heidi, and Ellen, thank you for watching our kids so Donna could join me in Spain.

Cambria, Joshua, and Olivia Gray, you are the most amazing children. You have influenced my words in these pages more than you will ever know. Thank you for the trust you have placed in me as your dad. The world will be a better place because of who you will each become. I love each of you and am a better man because of you.

Donna, thank you for your undying love and support and for believing in me even when I give you reason not to. You have been a rock in so many ways. I can never adequately thank you for all you are, but thank you for being an incredible mother, an amazing wife, and my partner in life. I fall more in love with you every day. You make me better in every way, and because of you, I get to see how much God loves me.

— FROM JUSTIN —

As a person living with a progressive neuromuscular disease, I've had to relearn a lot of things, learn a lot about myself, and let other people into my journey. The following individuals have been in my court for many years, serving, loving, and sharing life with me.

Chad and Jennifer Lansford: Though our paths don't cross anymore, you will always have a special place in my heart. I love you and miss you.

Jeff and Danielle Bolster: Thank you for always being there for us in San Diego, for laughter, and lots of fond memories.

Jim Johnson, my mentor: Since college, you have been my champion and prayer warrior. I am filled with joy every time we talk, and your heavenly insight has been invaluable in my life. Thank you.

My old college friends (now Idaho transplants) Ben and Joelle Powers, Mark and Melissa Michelson, Joe and Kelly Bankard, and new Idaho friends Leon and Carly Letson: Thank you for the laughs, love, and support. You made our transition to Idaho easier. Love you guys a ton.

My extended family, the Karlson crew: Gary and Maureen, Erik and Leticia, Marissa and Paris, and to all my nieces and nephews, your love and support for me and my marriage to Kirstin has meant the world. I love you and miss you.

My parents, Floyd "Jim" and Mavis Skeesuck: You have been amazing parents, and your unending love and support of all of my crazy ideas never ceases to amaze me. Thank you for continually praying for me and putting up with me as a kid. Remember, it was always Josie's fault.

Ryan, Tara, Jillian, and Zach Skeesuck: Thank you for your love and support throughout all of this. Ryan, thanks for your guidance, mentorship, and for being such an amazing big brother.

Josie and Timel Ragland: I can't thank you both enough for being behind me since day one of this whole crazy adventure. Josie, thanks for being the best little sister ever.

Jaden, Noah, and Lauren Skeesuck: You three are my light in this dark world. Thank you for being the kids God intended you to be and for loving me despite my disability. I hope this book can be something you can lean on when you feel you can't go forward in life. I love you all very much!

To Kirstin: I love living every day by your side. I thank God every day that I get the privilege of sharing life with you and exploring this world together. You have made me a better man, husband, and father to our three very independent children. I am blessed to have you in my life, loving me despite my faults and putting up with all of my crazy ideas, no matter how ridiculous they sound. I love you from head to toe, inside and out, and look forward to our next adventure together.

DISCUSSION GUIDE

1. Patrick and Justin have been friends their entire lives, witnessing each other's many trials and triumphs. Do you have a lifelong friend like this? How does this friendship differ from others in your life?

2. When Justin finally received his MAMA diagnosis, Patrick was quick to say, "Skeez, whatever you need, I'm here." In your trying times, how do your friends show up for you? What can you do to come alongside a needy friend this week?

3. Patrick's boss surprised him by allowing him to take time off for the Camino, even though it was much more time than someone in Patrick's position could usually take. And when Justin needed a specialized wheelchair, their

friends' company funded the entire cost. Have you ever
been the recipient of this kind of radical generosity? How
did you receive it?

4. Do you have an "impossible dream"? What are some steps
   you can take to make that dream a reality, to make the
   impossible possible?

5. Throughout the Camino, Justin and Patrick met travelers
   who, in their own way, were on the trail to push past
   whatever adversity they felt was holding them back.
   If you were to go on the Camino, what transformation
   would you seek?

6. On the first day of the Camino, it seemed as if everything
   went wrong—Patrick forgot his glasses, the terrain was
   steep and muddy, and Justin's wheelchair didn't survive
   the rough trail (which led to a host of other problems).
   Imagine yourself in their shoes: Would you give up on
   the trip, or keep going? Why?

7. In chapter 9, Patrick, Justin, and Ted decide to take a
   shortcut to avoid a particularly difficult part of the trail;
   yet, after hours of walking, they end up not far from where

they started. Have you ever failed to "measure twice, cut once"? What happened?

8. We see Patrick struggle to accept help from others throughout the Camino. Can you relate? What can you do to receive help from others more graciously?

9. What has Justin and Patrick's story taught you about the value of vulnerability? Of relationship? Of community?

10. In chapter 13, Patrick muses, "The Camino is filled with people who are dealing with something—searching for a safe place to face their demons. How different would the world be if every church offered that safe place?" What can you do today—even if it's a small step—to create a safe place in your church?

11. One of the most powerful moments on the Camino happens at the Cruz de Ferro, where Patrick leaves behind the burden of doing everything on his own. What burden do you need to leave behind today? How can you support others on their journeys?

NOTES

1. 1 Corinthians 13:4-7
2. See Matthew 22:37-39.
3. Matthew 25:35-40

ABOUT THE AUTHORS

BORN IN THE SAME small town just a couple of days apart, Justin Skeesuck and Patrick Gray are blessed with a unique relationship. Their childhood adventures and shared interests have made for many moments of laughter, joy, and treasured memories.

When they were fifteen years old, a car accident triggered a dormant disease in Justin's body, resulting in a life lived in a wheelchair.

Though life led Justin and Patrick down different paths and to colleges a thousand miles apart, their childhood friendship has not only survived, but has thrived in their adult years. Though their relationship has been put to the test by distance, time apart, and Justin's progressive neuromuscular disease, the two grow closer with each passing year and each new adventure.

In 2014, these lifelong friends did the impossible—together they tackled a five-hundred-mile pilgrimage through Spain known as the Camino de Santiago, or Way of St. James. While most people attempt this epic journey on foot, Justin traveled the entire distance in his wheelchair, pushed by Patrick (and others).

As Patrick physically pushed Justin over mountains, through deserts, and across fields, Justin pushed Patrick, mentally and emotionally, beyond fear and insecurity, into a whole new world of faith and freedom.

Their journey is a brilliant metaphor for the lives they have been blessed to live. Just as neither could have accomplished the rigorous trek on his own, their successes in life are largely attributed to the way they have pushed each other and the way they have allowed others to push them.

Now they work together, sharing unapologetic words of hope and faith through their writing and speaking, as they share the message that we can achieve more together.

Both men love music, road trips, and driving their wives crazy.

Justin lives in Eagle, Idaho, with his wife, Kirstin, and their three children: Jaden, Noah, and Lauren.

Patrick lives in nearby Meridian, Idaho, with his wife, Donna, and their three children: Cambria, Joshua, and Olivia.

LEARN MORE AT PUSHINC.US.

FOR FREE RESOURCES,
BONUS CONTENT, AND VIDEOS,
— VISIT US AT —
· ILLPUSHYOUBOOK.COM

IF YOU'RE INTERESTED IN HAVING US
SPEAK AT YOUR ORGANIZATION, SCHOOL, OR
SPECIAL EVENT, PLEASE VISIT PUSHINC.US.

CP1240

OUR JOURNEY ON THE CAMINO DE
SANTIAGO TRAIL WAS THE FOCUS OF THE
DOCUMENTARY I'LL PUSH YOU.

TO WATCH THE TRAILER AND LEARN
MORE ABOUT THE FILM, PLEASE VISIT:
ILLPUSHYOU.COM

CP1241